"ROUTE 66"
THE TELEVISION SERIES
1960–1964

JAMES ROSIN

James Rosin

Copyright © 2007 by James Rosin
All Rights Reserved

No part of this book may be reproduced in
any form or by any electronic or mechanical
means including information storage and
retrieval systems without permission in
writing from the publisher, except by
a reviewer who may quote brief
passages in a review.

Library of Congress Control Number 2006909728

ISBN 13: 978-0-9728684-2-6
ISBN 10: 0-9728684-2-9

Interior Design by Phyllis Pilla
Cover Graphics by Tina Marie Owens

Published by The Autumn Road Company
Philadelphia, PA

Printed by George H Buchanan
Bridgeport, NJ

Also by James Rosin

Philly Hoops: The SPHAS and WARRIORS

Rock, Rhythm and Blues

Philadelphia: City of Music

Naked City: The Television Series

Wagon Train: The Television Series

Adventures in Paradise: The Television Series

www.classictvseriesbooks.com

Herbert B. Leonard
"A man with a vision and a gifted collaborator."

**Stirling Silliphant, Howard Rodman,
Larry Marcus and Will Lorin**
Their humanity and
imagination was huge.

Sam Manners
He held it all together.

George and Marty
They found the music and the audience danced to it.

TABLE OF CONTENTS

Foreword x
Acknowledgments xi
Author's Note xii
Route 66, The Television Series 1
First Season:
   Episode Titles and Summaries 33
Second Season:
   Episode Titles and Summaries 65
Third Season:
   Episode Titles and Summaries 99
Fourth Season:
   Episode Titles and Summaries 133
Route 66 Production Company 158
Biographies 159
Endnotes 172
About the Author 173

FOREWORD

"Route 66" was one of the most unique American television dramas of the 1960s. The gritty social realism of the stories were enhanced by location shooting that encompassed the vast face of the country itself: from the glitter of Reno to the forests of Poland Spring, Maine, from the hill country near Austin, Texas to the skyscrapers of Chicago, the docks of Astoria, Oregon to the sails of Tampa Bay.

The road that Tod Stiles and Buz Murdock traveled in their search had two sides: one of optimism and another of dissatisfaction. The rearview mirror reflected what was left behind—pain, perhaps joy, but not the right fit; the horizon offered the possibility that the lack would be satisfied. The meaning would not be found in some finite goal at the end of the road, but in the discoveries along the way.

The show's black-and-white photography and spectacular locations provided a powerful backdrop to its downbeat stories and yielded a photographic and geographic realism that has never been duplicated on American television.

> Mark Alvey
> Media Historian

ACKNOWLEDGMENTS

I express my gratitude to the following people who took time to contribute to this book: George Maharis, Arthur Hiller, James Sheldon, Sam Manners, Richard Maynard, Mark Alvey, Nancy Malone, Anne Francis, Alvin Ganzer and Nehemiah Persoff. Also special thanks to Richard Maynard for his informative article in *Emmy* Magazine that I was able to use as primary source information; to Jerry Burton, editor of *Corvette Quarterly*; the article and interviews by Kermit Park in *Corvette Quarterly* that also provided me with insightful source information; Campbell-Ewald Publishing; *Chevrolet* Magazine; and to Colex Enterprises (a former joint venture of Columbia Pictures Television and the Lexington Broadcast Service) for providing me with photos and information about the series.

Photo credits: Colex Enterprises, James Sheldon, Nancy Malone and Nehemiah Persoff.

AUTHOR'S NOTE

Every attempt was made to ascertain the origin of each photo, which in some instances proved to be impossible. I express my gratitude to the original sources.

A conscientious effort was also made to ensure that each episode summary was as accurate as possible. Some episodes were unavailable for viewing. The summations for these shows were based on shooting scripts. These scripts may not contain certain minor plot details revised during filming. However, these revisions were again minor, and do not prevent the reader from a good understanding of the story line. Enjoy the book!

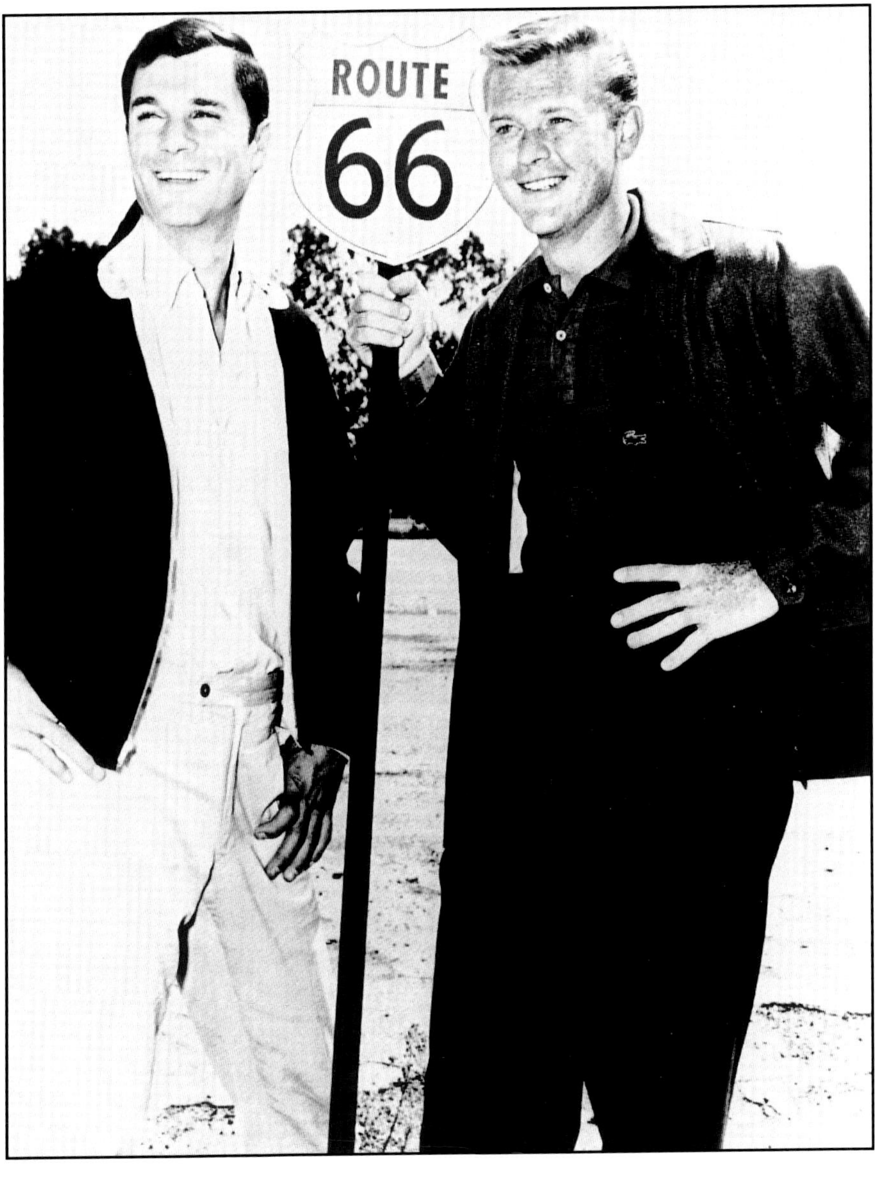
ROUTE
66

"ROUTE 66"
The Television Series
1960–1964

On Friday night, October 7, in the fall of 1960, "Route 66" debuted on the CBS Television Network. It was truly a very special television series about two young men from divergent backgrounds who traveled together (in a Corvette sports car) throughout the country, and along the way, encountered a myriad of fascinating characters and meaningful experiences. Their journey was amplified by Nelson Riddle's memorable music theme.

The show was created by producer Herbert B. Leonard and writer Stirling Silliphant. Leonard was a strong-willed, imaginative New Yorker who had worked his way up in the Hollywood film industry as a production and unit manager in over 50 low-budget films and action serials. From 1954 to 1959, he produced the beloved "Rin Tin Tin" series, affectionately remembered by every baby-boomer in America.

In 1958, Leonard was also the executive producer of "Naked City," a realistic 30-minute police drama set in New York City (based on the 1948 film classic) that starred John McIntire as the wise, veteran detective Muldoon, and James Franciscus as his young partner Jimmy Halloran. In the spring of 1959 the series was canceled by ABC.

One afternoon, Leonard and Silliphant (who wrote many of the 30-minute teleplays for "Naked City") were having lunch in a New York restaurant.

2 Route 66

HERBERT B. LEONARD
Executive Producer
"Naked City" and "Route 66"

I started reminiscing about how when I was a poor kid on the New York streets, I would pal around with a very wealthy prep school guy. I began to wonder out loud what it would have been like for a couple of complete opposites like the two of us to go traveling around the country in his sports car. Then I said something like "Stirling, that's our next show," and he jumped at it. By the time we stepped outside to get a cab, we were already working on the story for our pilot. We even knew who we wanted one of the leads to be. There was this young, outspoken actor we'd used on "Naked City," whom I believed had real star potential. His name was George Maharis.[1]

To test their idea, Leonard and Silliphant decided to incorporate a mini-pilot titled "Four Sweet Corners" into one of the later episodes of "Naked City." The storyline concerned two New York youths who team up to travel around the U.S. Maharis was cast as one of the characters. The other actor was Bobby Morris who died from a rare illness shortly after filming. The mini-pilot failed to attract attention, but when "Naked City" finished, Silliphant wrote the official one-hour pilot for "Route 66." Both Leonard and Silliphant agreed that the show would be filmed entirely on location to give it an unparalleled authenticity. But the script was rejected by Screen Gems (the television subsidiary of Columbia Pictures) who had co-produced the 30-minute version of "Naked City."

RICHARD MAYNARD
Producer, Author, Film Critic

At this point, Leonard made a very daring move. He put up his own money to shoot the pilot from a $350,000.00 bonus the studio owed him in exchange for 80% ownership of the show if it were picked up. With that began the process that launched a show that nobody wanted.[2]

MARK ALVEY
Media Historian

From the outset, the concept of "Route 66" (originally titled "The Searchers") was something quite different from the general run of network dramas at the time. Silliphant's proposal included a theme of "search, unrest, uncertainty, seeking answers and looking for a way of life." The characters would be "young enough to appeal to the youthful audience, old enough to be involved in adult situations." The stories would be "about something, honest, face up to life and look for and suggest meanings, things people can identify with, and yet there would be romance and escape of young people with wanderlust." The locales would encompass "the whole width and breadth of the U.S. with stories shot in the actual locations."[3]

The pilot episode was called "Black November" (originally titled "The Wolf Tree") and set in the fictional lumber camp town of Garth, Alabama. After scouting locations for about a month, the town of Concord, Kentucky was discovered and would represent Garth.

Back in New York, Leonard proceeded with casting the part of Tod Stiles. George Maharis had been cast as Buz Murdock, the dark-haired, brooding, street-smart orphan from Hell's kitchen. He had worked for Tod Stiles' father who owned a dockside shipping business and barge in Manhattan's East River. There he was befriended by Tod, an Ivy League kid from Yale, who worked with Buz during his summer vacations.

When the elder Stiles died of a sudden heart attack, Tod was left with a failed business. His only possession was a new Corvette. Now orphaned like Buz, Tod and he decided to take to the road to find themselves.

Casting the role of Tod was significant because he was the extreme opposite of Buz.

LEONARD

We needed an actor who could stand up to George on screen and off. It came down to two guys. One was Marty Milner, an experienced film actor, who had appeared in films like "Sweet Smell of Success," "Marjorie Morningstar" and "Gunfight at the OK Corral." The other candidate was a good-looking kid with some stage experience. We liked him, but he had a tendency to scream every time he got emotional. I used him in a guest shot later on, but we went with Milner. The name of the kid we didn't cast was Robert Redford.[1]

The pilot (filmed in February of 1960) had Tod and Buz stranded in the hostile, riverside town of Garth. When their car breaks down, aid is refused them at every turn. Finally, after the town tyrant agrees to have their car fixed, Tod is roughed up and kidnapped. In Buz's quest to find his partner, both he and Tod discover the town's deep, dark secret that almost gets them lynched.

The show was powerfully written, complemented by a strong guest cast, and CBS bought the series. Screen Gems would co-produce the show sponsored in part by Chevrolet.

After "Route 66" was sold, "Naked City" was renewed by ABC as an hour-long series for the 1960-61 season. Paul Burke, as Detective Adam Flint, joined the cast which included Horace McMahon, Harry Bellaver, and Nancy Malone. The show would be shot entirely in Manhattan and the surrounding boroughs.

MAYNARD

Leonard was now producing two network television series with very difficult location situations that divided his attention. Much of the responsibility for producing "Route 66" was given to veteran production manager, Sam Manners, and Stirling Silliphant.[2]

SAM MANNERS
Executive in Charge of Production
ROUTE 66

There's never been a show like "Route 66." We were always under pressure, always close to missing deadlines—though we never did. Stirling would pick locations from the map, interesting places where events were happening, like a big cattle auction in Reno, or a major harvest. Both he and I would visit these places

MANNERS (Cont'd)

and check them out. Then Stirling, or a writer he chose, would build a story around Tod and Buz in that place. It was my job to supervise the shooting. I had a permanent crew of about 60 people, most of whom were with us for the entire four year run of the show.[1]

From 1960-1964, "Route 66" traveled to 24 states throughout the country including Kentucky, Georgia, Louisiana, Florida, Texas, Tennessee, Missouri, Colorado, Utah, New Mexico, Nevada, Arizona, California, Oregon, Montana, Minnesota, Illinois, Ohio, Pennsylvania, Maryland, New York, Massachusetts, Maine and Vermont. (The show also filmed in Toronto.)

MANNERS

We would make a particular place like, say, Pittsburgh, our base for about three shows and we'd shoot one in the city, and two in the rural areas within a 50-mile radius. Then we'd move on in the same pattern. We avoided serious weather problems by shooting in warmer climates in winter and moving north in summer. We trucked everything from place to place and when "Route 66" visited a city, it was a big event like a circus coming to town. We always received a huge welcome. I raised my kids on the road with that show as did some of the other crew. We even employed a full-time teacher to travel with us named Nora Choate who taught Shirley Temple. The 60 of us, including Marty and George, were a family.[1,6]

MARTIN MILNER
Series Co-Star

I liked the fact that we were pioneering a very innovative way to make television— to do it on the road in the actual locations. We were doing something no one else had ever done, or has really done since. The one sad thing is that we weren't in color, because we were in so many beautiful spots, like being in New England in the fall when the leaves were changing.[4]

Because the show was filmed in black and white, all of the Corvettes used had to be a color that was compatible with the lighting scheme.

GEORGE MAHARIS
Series Co-Star

A lot of people are under the impression that the Corvette was red. It never was. It was powder blue in the pilot and early episodes, then it was beige for the run of the series. They found that the blue color shot in black-and-white would reflect too much light. They couldn't balance enough light on Marty and me, and the result was we were silhouetted in the shot. When they used the beige Corvette, that color absorbed more light and cast less reflection. Dark colors absorb more light. Consequently, while I was working, I would get the sunburn and Marty wouldn't.[5]

MANNERS

Every 3000 miles, we would turn in the Corvettes we used on the show and get new ones. We probably went through 3-4 cars

MANNERS (Cont'd)

each season. We put more mileage on the Corvettes given to us by Chevrolet for personal use than the ones used on the show.[6]

ALVEY

The Corvette which Leonard and Silliphant referred to as the "third character" is an interested and conflicted symbol. In one sense, it's bound up in the meaning of the nation's postwar "love affair" with the automobile. It's a sports car with a powerful engine and only two seats signifying speed, mobility and independence. Yet in the series, it's sometimes put to work as a winch, towing a trailer, or pulling a mule. It's an expensive convertible, a status symbol, but it's Tod's only asset and his single memento of his father; he must drive forklifts and pitch hay to put gas in it. The Corvette and its occupants manifest a curious mix of the bourgeois and the beat.[3]

Filming outdoors on location presented a few technical problems but nothing unsolvable.

MANNERS

The scenes with Tod and Buz conversing in the car while driving were done by towing the car behind a station wagon carrying the camera crew. Cameras were also attached to the sides for close-ups or over-the-shoulder shots for each side of the Corvette. For rear angle shots, we used a Chevy Corvair. That car had the trunk in front and engine in the rear. So we removed the trunk lid, mounted cameras in the trunk, then filmed the scene while we followed the Corvette.[6]

An interesting example of this was the ending of the episode "Birdcage on My Foot," where director Elliot Silverstein has the camera follow the Corvette meandering through the Boston streets as Tod and Buz escort addict Arnie (portrayed by Robert Duvall) to a U.S. Public Health Hospital.

Directing an episode of the show was not without inherent problems.

RICHARD MAYNARD

There was simply never an adequate amount of time for a director to become familiar with locations or work closely with his actors. Shooting schedules were usually six days and production often lagged because scripts were not ready to be filmed. Nevertheless, some directors apparently coped well with these pressures, and people like Arthur Hiller, Elliot Silverstein, David Lowell Rich and Tom Gries were given their starts on "Route 66" and worked the show frequently. Leonard used other talented directors but they couldn't work under the tight deadlines.[2]

LEONARD

Robert Altman and Sam Peckinpah were very talented men we tried who didn't work out. They changed their scripts and we had no time for creative differences or midnight inspirations. The directors and I discussed a script before they left for locations. If they had contributions and changes to make, that was the time. Our deadlines didn't permit tinkering with the script during filming.[1]

ARTHUR HILLER
Director: Multiple Episodes

Every episode was a challenge physically. TV is a medium of compromises because you have little time. The trick is to know where you can compromise and where you can't.[7]

ALVIN GANZER
Director: Multiple Episodes

TV is tough because you always have a lot to do in little time. The clock is always ticking. "Route 66" was difficult because of all the different places you had to travel to and work in. But those of us that worked the show on a regular basis adapted and came as well prepared as possible. It also helped that we had an exceptional crew.[8]

NANCY MALONE
Guest Star: First Class Mouliak; Naked City Co-Star, 1960-63

The crews on both "Route 66" and "Naked City" were terrific. They rose to the challenge of getting actors to locations and acclimated to their surroundings, their co-workers, props, wardrobe, everything. That was sometimes a difficult task and they always made it work.[9]

MAHARIS

Our crew did some innovative things in those days. On long trucking shots, they couldn't use a boom mike that would show in frame. So they'd attach these tiny mics to our clothes, conceal them, and snake the wires up, around and down the inside of our pants leg,

MAHARIS (Cont'd)

pulling the wires back as we moved along so they wouldn't be visible. That allowed the camera crew to do these long trucking shots and widen as they pulled back, getting in a lot of scenery. It also enabled us to shoot on location and seldom have to loop our lines in a studio.[5]

JAMES SHELDON
Director: Multiple Episodes

The challenge of directing "Route 66" was adjusting to the environment you were working in, that varied week-to-week. Sometimes you'd get a complete script in advance, but it didn't always work out that way. When I first began working on the show, I was used to working at a studio where you could fix things. If you were shooting a scene that wasn't working, you could call the producer or writer, they'd come down on the set and work with you to remedy the situation. But on location, you'd have to adjust to your surroundings, make decisions and be creative. Working with Jack Marta, the director of photography, was a great learning experience. Jack taught me what locations were best to shoot. For example, which side of the street was the sun on, or the right angle if there was a contrast with shadow and sun so you didn't shoot into it.[10]

MAHARIS

Jack Marta was a very creative man. What I also liked about him was, if there was a problem, you could talk to him; he'd listen and

MAHARIS (Cont'd)

work it out. In the early days of the show, they used spot lights on the floor of the Corvette that would strike us from an upward angle. It didn't look right. The sun doesn't come from under your chin. When I mentioned it to Jack, he went out and got these small quartz lights, and placed them on the metal strip where the convertible top meets the top of the car. That way it looked like the light was coming from the sun and it appeared much more natural.[5]

SHELDON

Despite the challenges and problems we faced, the show was a very well-run operation. If I ever had a problem or disagreement with anyone, I could always get Bert [Leonard] on the phone via Sam [Manners]. I had instant access to him and he would solve any existing difficulty. Bert was very smart, hired the right people and delegated authority well.[10]

ALVEY

Any tribulations of production on the road were soon eclipsed by aggravation from the network executives. CBS TV President Jim Aubrey wanted more "broads, bosoms and fun." He complained that the series was too downbeat and warned that the network would discontinue its association with the show if the production continued to disregard their repeated suggestions.[3]

Leonard and Silliphant had creative control and although they went along with Aubrey to some degree, their attempt to lighten the show subsided after several episodes.

The Television Series 13

ALVEY

Leonard had the sponsors on his side who liked the hard-hitting show they bought based on the pilot. As he said, "they wanted the reality, the drama, and the movement; not the sexy women and cliché characters."

Despite the adverse conditions of producing and directing a weekly series on the road, and conflicts with the network, "Route 66" became a successful television show.

As the series progressed, the unique ingredient of filming on location all over the country was enhanced by honest and literate writing by Stirling Silliphant, and others such as Howard Rodman, Will Lorin and Larry Marcus. The emphasis was on character development, and the premise of "Route 66" enabled Tod and Buz to encounter an endless variety of people and circumstances in their travels: a relentless Nazi hunter in the Gulf of Mexico; drought-stricken ranchers in Zion National Park; a psychotic killer on the slopes of Squaw Valley; a down-trodden boxer in Youngstown, Ohio; a dying blues singer in Pittsburgh; a revolutionary terrorist in Boston; and an orphaned Bar Mitzvah boy in Phoenix, to name a few.

HILLER

Stirling was able to write a great variety of stories. Sometimes they were gentle, people stories, other times suspenseful or controversial. But each of them was different; sometimes 180 degrees apart. So the audience tuning in every week would watch something new. I remember shooting an episode in New Mexico called "The Newborn," with Albert Dekker and Robert Duvall. It dealt with a native Indian girl about to give birth to a

HILLER (Cont'd)

rancher's son. Here we were doing a western that dealt with values and controversy that made for good drama and had something to say. Another episode called "The Clover Throne" with Jack Warden, dealt with a man's efforts to stop construction of a road across his property—a situation still timely today.[7]

MILNER

Stirling always had a finger on the pulse of what was happening before the general public seemed to know. We did a show on LSD called "The Thin White Line" when nobody really knew what LSD was. I had certainly never heard of it, but Stirling had. I think he was kind of in the vanguard on things like that and Bert Leonard had the good sense to go along with him. I felt we were breaking new ground. I was always happy with the storylines—most of them anyway.[4]

Fortunately, Milner and Maharis had a lot of input when it came to character development.

MILNER

Anyone doing a series has input as far as characters go. If something arose at a location and we didn't like it, all we had to do was get on the phone. We didn't always win those fights, but we had the opportunity to voice our opinion.[4]

MAHARIS

There were times when we had problems with the script. I remember one time at Riverside [raceway in California] we were do-

MAHARIS (Cont'd)

ing an episode called "The Quick and the Dead," during the first season. The script read that Marty was racing the Corvette and I was against it. I thought that was wrong. I said, "I'm not his mother," because the script was making me sound like I was protective of him. Buz would simply say, "Go for it," and help him. He'd be behind him 100 percent. He'd wish he could do it himself, but he wouldn't stop someone else. That's the whole reason to be on the road; to go out and discover, to take chances. They finally decided that my version was more in line with the character.[4]

Initially, "Route 66" was billed as an action-adventure series by CBS, but even in the first season there were many episodes where there was more emphasis on character contribution to the storyline and less on plot and circumstance. "Ten Drops of Water" involves Tod and Buz with Vergil and Helen Page as they fight to hold onto the drought-ridden ranch their family has owned for over a hundred years. In "Legacy for Lucia," they help Lucia Trapani raise money to buy a new Madonna for her town's church. "Trap at Cordova" finds the pair educating children in a small and secluded New Mexico town controlled by a man who refuses to let them leave.

ALVEY

As Silliphant suggested, "Route 66" was oriented toward the stories of the various souls encountered by Tod and Buz in their stops along the highway. The guest stars would serve as episodic protagonists while their motives drove the narrative.[3]

Two examples are "Incident on a Bridge" which involves Tod and Buz in a haunting "beauty and the beast" tale told in flashbacks, and "First Class Mouliak" about the discordant relationships between Jack, a Russian laborer (superbly played by Nehemiah Persoff) and his son Janosh (portrayed by Robert Redford) and the near tragic results that ensue. Both are powerful dramas with a strong guest cast that brings them to life.

ALVEY

Even in stories where Tod and Buz's involvement is marginal, they serve a crucial function. As outsiders in the community and conflicts through which they pass, they serve to generate insights into the motivations of the characters they encounter. In their efforts to help and support their troubled acquaintances, they provide answers which would not be available without their perspective.[3]

In other storylines, the goals of Tod and Buz are directly linked to the intentions of the main characters. "Like a Motherless Child" explores Buz's attachment to Hanna Ellis, a middle-aged woman whose son was taken from her years before. In "Most Vanquished, Most Victorious," Tod searches for his cousin Carole, based on a promise to his dying Aunt Kitty. "The Opponent," has Buz drawn to his boyhood friend, now a worn-out fighter.

ALVEY

Episodes like "The Mud Next," "The Thin White Line," "Even Stones Have Eyes," and "Fifty Miles From Home," are interesting and distinctive in so far as they provide closer and

ALVEY (Cont'd)

more sustained explorations of the emotional make-up of Tod, Buz and later, Linc.[3]

NEHEMIAH PERSOFF
Guest Star: "Incident On a Bridge" and "First Class Mouliak"

I appreciated the writing because it was so honest and truthful. There was a realism that the writers captured, that made it easy to act. When we were filming "Incident" in the Russian Hill section of Cleveland, I portrayed a Neanderthal-looking man with bulging teeth. There was a newspaperman from the Soviet Union covering the shoot. He asked to interview me, and I was uncomfortable speaking to him with the false teeth I was wearing for the role. Yet I was also uncomfortable taking them out in his presence. So I stayed in character. The newspaperman became even more uncomfortable than me, thinking he was interviewing the actual character that Stirling wrote in his script.[11]

SHELDON

We always had very good actors on the show. Bert had a great casting director in New York named Marion Dougherty, who always presented you with good people. That was a blessing when you were on location, moving quickly, and didn't have a lot of rehearsal time to work with actors.[10]

MALONE

Marion Dougherty was the queen of casting directors. She had an extraordinary eye for talent and always cast for chemistry. That's something you don't see as much of today when they put a cast together. I also think that we actors in those days had a great pride in what we did. We knew that we were working with exceptional writers and very talented and creative people. We certainly didn't have the accommodations that a lot of series stars have today. I don't recall having a dressing room on "Naked City" until they brought in a "honeywagon" for the final season. I would dress in storefront windows before people came to work. But we didn't seem to mind. We were thrilled to be doing a hit show and adapted to most of the inconveniences.[9]

Each week, a gifted array of performers helped bring these multi-dimensional characters to life. Along with Nehemiah Persoff in the premiere season, they included: Everett Sloane, Patty McCormack, Keir Dullea, Janice Rule, Thomas Gomez, Betty Field, Henry Hull, Lew Ayres, Suzanne Pleshette, E. G. Marshall, Jay C. Flippen, Charles McGraw, Bethel Leslie, Inger Stevens, Edgar Buchanan, Edward Binns, Leslie Nielsen, Conrad Nagel, Lee Marvin, Anne Francis, Jack Lord, Michael Rennie, Dorothy Malone, Ben Johnson, Sylvia Sidney, Walter Mathau, Beatrice Straight, Dan Duryea, Robert Duvall, Darren McGavin, Ed Asner, and Susan Oliver.

ANNE FRANCIS
Guest Star: "Play It Glissando" and "A Month of Sundays"

"Route 66" was a great idea that worked. I really enjoyed doing the show. I think when you have a pair of characters that travel throughout the country, meet new people, and get involved in different situations, you have something that's very unique and interesting.[12]

Another significant reason for the success of "Route 66" was Milner and Maharis. They were perfectly cast and became at one with their roles as the series progressed.

MILNER

I think they wrote the characters and they found the actors who fit them. But any time you do a series, as it goes along, the characters often become more and more like the person—the actor. You might do a certain thing one week and do it really well because it's close to you, it's easy for you to play. And without realizing it, the writers will write that again. They'll say, "Remember when George did this and how good it was? Let's write a thing like that for him again." So over the life of a show, even if it doesn't start out that way, it often involves characters that become pretty close to the actors who are playing them.[4]

MAHARIS

You usually try to bring an actor into a role who has the style and emotional power that you want. I was very close to Buz. I was a per-

MAHARIS (Cont'd)

son who was raised in the streets of New York, and I was primarily a person who reacted with his gut. Marty was educated differently than I was. We were very different.[4]

SHELDON

Marty and George were completely different personalities. Marty had been an actor since he was a kid. He was very experienced and professional. He was more "Let's get it done." George was more of a thinking person and would sometimes put the director to the test. I can remember we were shooting a show in Tucson, Arizona called "You Never Had It So Good." Peter Graves and Patricia Barry were the guest leads. There was a scene where George gets out of a car, walks up to a hotel and goes inside to the front desk. So we shot it once, and it took a long time. So I said to George, "That's fine, but can we do it a little faster," and he barked back, "What kind of direction is that?" I saw there was going to be a problem, so I said to my camera crew, "Listen, I hate to make you do this, but can we go outside and get a quick cut-away close-up of Patricia waiting in the car?" Which would take the pause out. So George came up to me later and said, "You really know how to handle me, don't you?" Honestly, I didn't do what I did to handle George. I was simply trying to solve a problem. The way the shot was laid out, it took a long time for him to get from the car to the desk. Incidentally, George and I got along very well after that and became the best of friends.[10]

GANZER

I never had a problem with either George or Marty. They were very willing actors who went out of their way to give me what I needed. I think the show succeeded because they were not only skilled actors but very likable personalities. That's very important when you're doing a weekly series. I also think the contrast between them worked to their advantage.[8]

HILLER

It's true Marty and George were very different, yet they played off each other so well and always maintained a good sense of their individuality, even though they were together a lot, sharing common values and helping others. They were also very open to thoughts and suggestions about what we were doing; and I would listen to them as well. It's true a director has to maintain a vision about the story you're telling on film. But you also have to keep an open ear as you go along. If one person says something you haven't thought of, it's been worth listening. The thing I liked about doing the series was that it was a team effort and group activity.[7]

FRANCIS

George and Marty were great to work with, and I later did a film with George called "The Satan Bug." I also loved working with Arthur Hiller, a gentle, kind, lovely man who had such an ease about him, and that made us comfortable to express whatever we were feeling. Ironically, when we were filming "A Month of Sundays" in Montana, Arthur was into leg

FRANCIS (Cont'd)

wrestling. One day he challenged me and I won—I guess because I was three months pregnant at the time and had two extra legs on my side![12]

MALONE

George and Marty were distinctly different. George was the bad boy. He had this dangerous element about him which was very attractive; this dark, smoldering sexuality. Marty was the adorable and wholesome one who held everything together. In certain ways they were like oil and water; but the overall result was that they were fabulous together.[9]

PERSOFF

Marty and George knew they had a good thing going and were very serious about their work. In both shows I did with them, they were constantly working toward a desired result which was my main focus as well. I thoroughly enjoyed doing the show.[11]

Maharis was dynamic as the intense, brooding, sometimes explosive Buz Murdock. Yet he also brought a compassion and vulnerability to the character that was compelling. This was aptly shown in season two in an episode entitled "The Mud Nest" where his search for the mother that deserted him leads Buz to a Baltimore hospital and an emotional reckoning.

MAHARIS

When we were shooting "Mud Nest" in a rural part of Maryland, I had a fight scene

MAHARIS (Cont'd)

with the man who was actually my stunt double. At one point, my head was on the ground, and when he swung at me, he had no room and caught me flush on the mouth. My lip was bruised, bloody and swollen, so they took me to a nearby doctor. I never bothered to change my clothes which were ripped and dirty from rolling on the ground. So the doctor who had never seen the show took one look at me and said, "I don't treat bums."[5]

More episodes filmed in the second season provided revelations about Buz Murdock and showcased Maharis's acting ability. In "Birdcage on My Foot," his relentless determination to help a heroin addict (expertly played by Robert Duvall) reveals a hidden part of his life. In "Even Stones Have Eyes," as Buz regains his sight after being blinded in a construction accident, Maharis is at one with the character. In "City of Wheels" his anger and frustration at his inability to help a cynical paraplegic, reveal a wrath that is also a sign of his vulnerability.

MAHARIS

"Route 66" was the chance to do something I believed in; a chance to express things that I felt from the standpoint of the character that I played and the way I believed this character lived his life. That was very important to me.[4]

Maharis adhered to this credo, and on occasion it became necessary to challenge a new director who had his own interpretation.

MAHARIS

I didn't always agree with a director's point of view, but if it had merit, I would work with

MAHARIS (Cont'd)

him and contribute as much as I could. However, when someone insisted on doing something that was contrary to my character, and not good for the show, I would speak up. One time this director came on the show and wanted to portray Buz as a guy who knew nothing about music. I explained to him that we had recently done a show with Ethel Waters about a dying blues singer where Buz displayed a keen knowledge of music. So it made no sense to contradict that. Well, this director didn't want to hear it. In fact, he got nasty, and said, "I'm the director and you'll do it my way." So I told him, "You can do it your way, but you'll do it without me, because I'm walking off the show." The end result was Bert Leonard got involved and straightened the guy out.[5]

As an affable and reliable Tod Stiles, Milner displayed a solid acting ability. Examples are his impassioned speech to a New Mexico legislature in support of a small town in "Trap at Cordova"; his odyssey as a drug-induced psychotic in "The Thin White Line"; as well as his purpose and resolve to even the odds with a violent impresario (played by Lee Marvin) in "Mon Petit Chou," to name a few.

MANNERS

I can remember in "Mon Petit Chou" the script builds to this climactic fight scene. When we shot it, Marty accidentally splattered Lee Marvin's nose wide open. Unfortunately, Lee moved to his left instead of his right, and Marty hit him flush with a right hand. The doctor had to put 20 stitches in Marvin's nose

MANNERS (Cont'd)

to patch him up, and then we couldn't shoot anything but long shots until his nose healed. Ironically, Marty and Lee Marvin were friendly and had worked together before Route 66.[4,6]

In the spring of 1962, near the end of season two, George Maharis contracted hepatitis and missed the final four episodes.

MAHARIS

We were doing a favorite episode of mine called "Even Stones Have Eyes" where I'm accidentally blinded. In fact, when I knew I was going to play blind, I used opaque contact lenses so the reality would be better for me and the people watching the show. I worked very long hours and at one point we were still shooting at 4 in the morning with two shots left to do. In this particular scene, I was supposed to rescue actress Barbara Barrie who had fallen into a river. It was a very cold night and the water was freezing. So they gave us both wet suits to wear. Barbara was wearing a trench coat so that was no problem for her. But my jacket and trousers wouldn't fit over the wet suit and my clothes had to match the previous shots. So I went into the water unprotected. You could see the steam coming off my jacket on camera. I began to get sick but I kept on working. The next thing I knew, we were filming an episode in Catalina which was basically a two-character story with Joanna Moore and myself. Again, it was a very lengthy, physical show and I was in and out of the

MAHARIS (Cont'd)

water for much of the shoot. At one point when I looked in the mirror, the whites of my eyes were yellow. Everyone told me I looked fine and I didn't realize how sick I was. With a month left of shooting, I finally saw a doctor. He took one look at me and put me in the hospital right away. I had hepatitis.[5]

Silliphant and story supervisor Howard Rodman tried to circumvent Maharis' absence by writing four scripts that featured controversy, suspense and strong characterizations. In "Hello and Goodbye," Tod meets and falls for a beautiful blonde, unaware that she has a dual personality. "A Feat of Strength" finds Tod working as an assistant to a wrestling promoter who brings a proud Hungarian champion to the U.S. under false pretenses. "Hell's Empty, All the Devils Are Here" has Tod employed by a man who plots a murderous revenge, and "From an Enchantress Fleeing" focuses on an inventor and his wife (whom Tod assists) in a human story about compulsion for success and its disastrous effect on their marriage.

When Maharis returned for the third year, "Route 66" was an established success, and season three began with momentum.

"One Tiger to a Hill" (filmed in the coastal town of Astoria, Oregon) featured David Janssen as an embittered and irrational veteran with a vengeful attitude toward Tod. "Journey to Nineveh" was an offbeat comedy with silent screen star Buster Keaton. "Ever Ride the Waves in Oklahoma?" follows Buz's efforts to bring down a "surfer king" that almost costs him his life in the balance. "Voice at the End of the Line" is a heartwarming story about Buz and Tod's efforts to help a distraught stock clerk meet the woman of his dreams, and "Lizard Leg and Owlet's

Wings" finds Tod and Buz involved with Boris Karloff (who appears as the Frankenstein monster), Lon Chaney, Jr. (who appears as the Wolfman), and Peter Lorre at a hotel convention in Chicago.

MANNERS

We were shooting a scene with actual caskets in the lobby of the O'Hare Inn in Chicago, where we filmed most of the show. Then Boris Karloff, who was dressed as the Frankenstein monster, walked into the men's room and scared the hell out of a couple of unsuspecting guests. I'll never forget the look on their faces when they came out of that bathroom.[4,6]

Close to the midway point of the third season, George Maharis experienced a recurring bout of hepatitis and began to miss shows.

MAHARIS

When I came back for the third year, I came back much too soon. I was in the hospital for 3 1/2 weeks and then I went back to work. I remember an executive at Chevrolet developed hepatitis about the same time I did. He was out of work for five months, then went back to work for two days a week. No one went back to work as soon as I did. But I was told that when I returned, I would only have to work 3-4 hours a day and if I didn't come back, the show would not get picked up by the network for another season. Although I was supposed to work a limited number of hours each day, it never worked out that way. I was heavily involved in the storylines, so I worked about 70 hours the first week, 68 hours the next week, 80 hours the following week, and so

MAHARIS (Cont'd)

on. With a few exceptions that went on for much of the first thirteen episodes. I wasn't feeling well, but I kept pushing. By the time we got to St. Louis to shoot an episode called "Hey Moth, Come Eat the Flame," I had nothing left. I went to the doctor and was told I was having a relapse. He said, "You need to leave the show, go home and rest. If you don't, you're going to get cirrhosis of the liver, and the next step is death." The press said I wanted out of the series so I could concentrate on a movie career. That wasn't true. I loved doing the show. I didn't want to leave. That's why I came back in the first place. But if I didn't exit when I did, I would have done irreparable damage to my health.[5]

MAYNARD

Leonard filed a breach-of-contract suit against Maharis to try and force him to finish the season. The actor never returned to the show and the suit was settled out of court. As it turned out, Maharis didn't work for almost two years.[2]

Initially, Tod was shown making phone calls to Buz who was hospitalized with a virus in California. Ultimately, there was no mention of Buz in the scripts or credits, and his departure was never explained. Perhaps the producers hoped he would eventually return.

Milner appeared in a total of 9 episodes by himself, but the show could not continue with single character storylines. So Silliphant wrote a script introducing a character named Lincoln Case who was similar in nature to Buz. Case was a conflicted hero of the Vietnam struggle with an explosive nature.

In his debut episode, "50 Miles from Home," Private First Class Linc Case arrives in Houston, and attempts to brush off a girl who's been following him. His actions are resented by a group of college basketball players being coached by Tod. Linc offers no resistance when they start pushing him around. However, when they trip him, he falls and gashes his head. Linc explodes, using martial arts and wades into the group, maiming one of the boys for life.

Tod seeks revenge. Fighting to a draw, Linc and Tod come to respect each other. At first Linc hopes to return home, but then realizes he needs time to find himself, and drives away with Tod.

MAYNARD

Silliphant's script created a potentially fascinating new character. Post-Vietnam Syndrome was a problem we later became very much aware of. Linc Case had none of the rowdy charm or street-smart nerve of Buz Murdock. Whoever played Linc would have to bring a lot of natural instinct to the part in order to contrast with Milner's Tod Stiles.[2]

LEONARD

I knew just the actor who could have made Linc work. He was a featured player in "Gunsmoke." He played a blacksmith named Quint Asper and he had a very powerful presence. He was Burt Reynolds and we tried everything to sign him. But he didn't want to be another actor's replacement.[1]

Leonard was forced to look elsewhere and ultimately settled for a young actor named Glenn Corbett who was under contract to Columbia. Corbett was handsome and a bit rugged-looking, but his personality and acting persona was much closer to Martin Milner. The chemistry and stark contrast that existed between Maharis and Milner was a key element to the success of "Route 66" and the show suffered without it.

SHELDON

Stirling wrote a very interesting character in Buz Murdock. George made Buz fascinating and Marty provided the perfect balance. Glenn was a handsome guy and a very competent actor. But he didn't have the spark that George did, and his on-screen personality was much closer to Marty's.[10]

LEONARD

We knew when George left the show it was over. But we had our audience and the network and sponsor renewed us for a fourth season with Marty and Glenn. Eventually though, the audience got bored with us which was to be expected. It's sad when you think about the show's potential. The people at Chevrolet and I had been discussing taking Tod and Buz to Europe after the fourth season. "Route 66" could have been the first American series shot abroad. After all, a year after we folded, "I Spy" actually accomplished that. I think if George had stayed, we would have run for years.[1]

The series ended with a two-parter, filmed in Tampa, Florida. It aired on March 6 and March 13 in 1964. In "Where There's A Will, There's A Way," Tod Stiles meets and marries Margo Tiffin (played by Barbara Eden) and Linc Case returns to Texas.

Beginning in late March of that year, "Route 66" went into reruns for six months with CBS airing selected episodes with Milner and Maharis from the first three seasons. The show aired its final rerun in September of 1964.

HILLER

I think what was significant about the show is that you had two young men who cared. Yes, they were traveling, searching and looking for work. Yet in many of the stories they showed compassion and concern for other people. I think that may have opened up people watching the show to care about others and not worry about themselves all the time. In the early '60s we were still very self-absorbed and "Route 66" showed a togetherness that was affecting.[7]

ALVEY

A very special thing about the series was the attempt to forge the connection between people, the relationships that often seem so difficult to build and maintain, but are so essential to social life. The stories didn't argue that love conquers all or that every problem could be solved by well-meaning heroes. The show acknowledged as Buz did, "that every one of us is born into solitary confinement and we spend the rest of our lives sending out a small S.O.S. we hope someone will hear."[3]

Many television fans of "Route 66" feel there could never be another show like it. Stirling Silliphant summed it up best:

SILLIPHANT

We were able to show the American character on that show with all kinds of people in every kind of situation that gave us a special richness. That would be difficult to show today since the country's become more homogenized. Regional differences are fading. There are more and more Holiday Inns and freeways.

"Route 66" I believe really did influence a generation. The General Motors people gave us some fascinating profiles of our audiences from 1960-64. We had a huge share of very young kids ages 10-14. Our shows were about young people searching for their identities, confronting conflicting values, frustrations, anger, hope. That whole generation of kids that watched us every Friday night became the college-age protesters of the late sixties. I've got to believe that Tod and Buz were early expressions of that generation.[1]

Tod Stiles (Martin Milner) and Buz Murdock (George Maharis) in 1960, about to begin their journey. Their travels would take them all over the country where they'd experience a myriad of characters and meaningful experiences.

Tod and Buz cross the river into the town of Garth where trouble awaits them in "Black November," the pilot episode telecast on October 7, 1960.

George Maharis and Martin Milner in a publicity shot with Patty McCormack, guest star in "Black November," originally titled "The Wolf Tree."

Janice Rule and George Maharis in a scene from "A Lance of Straw," filmed in Grand Isle, Louisiana in July of 1960. This was the first show filmed after CBS viewed the pilot and bought the series.

While Milner was usually accommodating, Maharis was intense and sometimes took a director to task.

George Maharis and Anne Francis during filming of "A Month of Sundays," in Butte, Montana. The bittersweet love story was the premiere episode of season two in September of 1961.

Martin Milner and Julie Newmar in a scene from "How Much a Pound is Albatross?" which aired during the series second year. Newmar's off-beat character, Vickie Russell, would return the following season in "Give an Old Cat a Tender Mouse."

George Maharis and Simon Oakland rehearse a scene for "To Walk with a Serpent," a political thriller filmed in Boston in the fall of 1961. The controversial episode concerned a revolutionary terrorist who plans to blow up a historical monument.

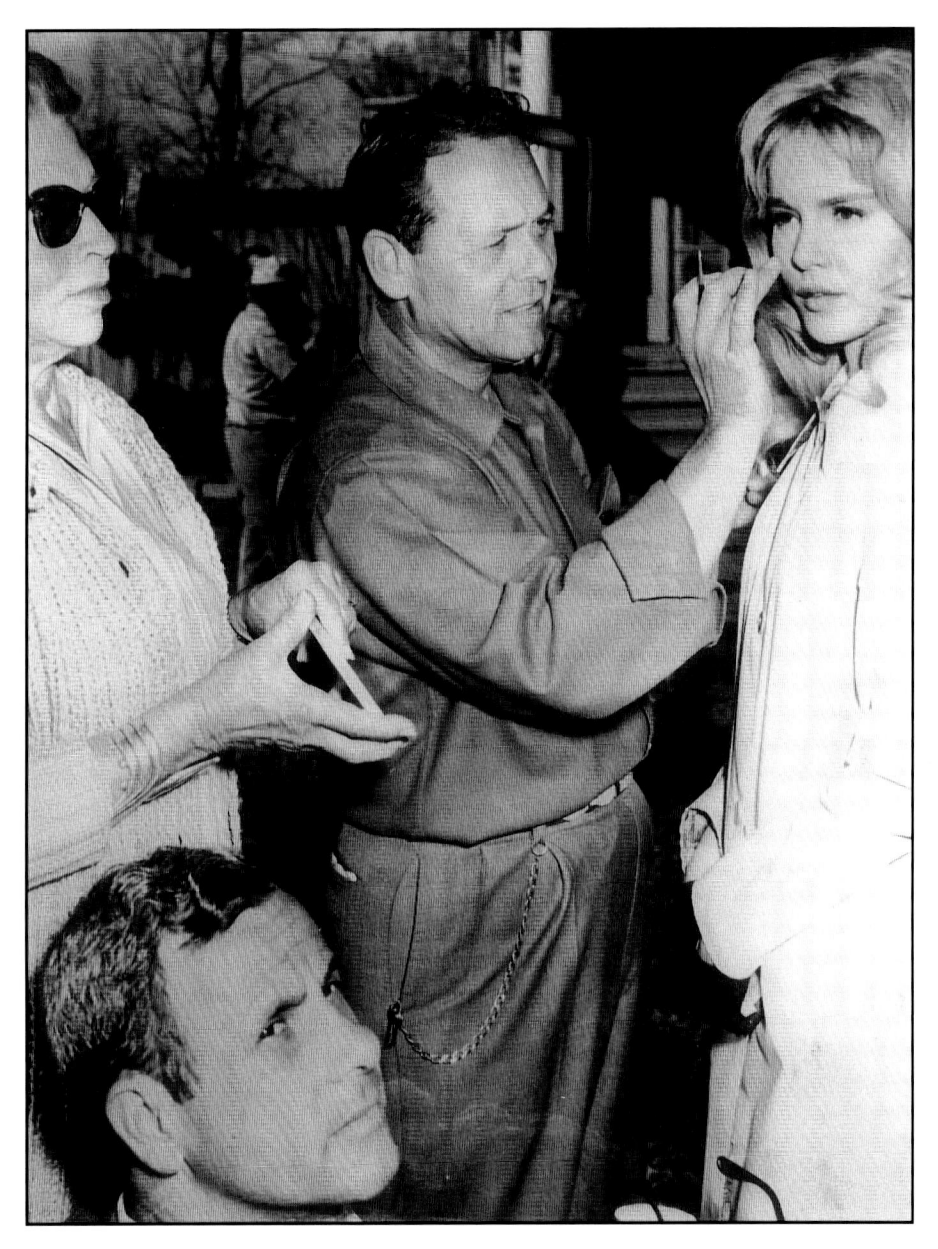

Actress Tuesday Weld gets a touchup from makeup man Abe Haberman prior to shooting a scene for "Love is a Skinny Kid," filmed in Lewisville, Texas. Director James Sheldon is seated at the bottom of the photo. The drama also featured Cloris Leachman and Burt Reynolds. It aired on April 6, 1962.

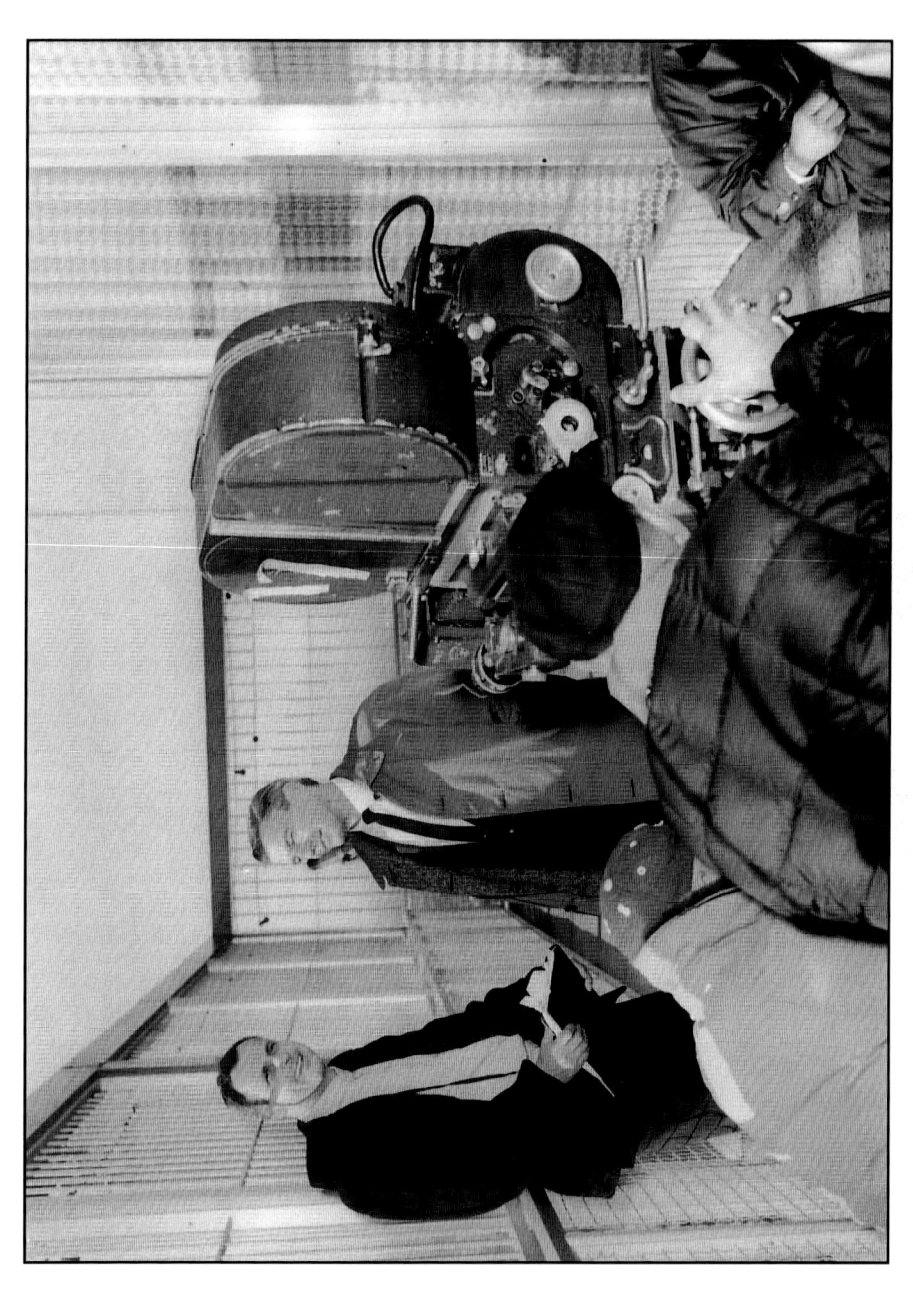

Jack Marta and his camera crew compose a single shot of guest star David Wayne shown conversing with director James Sheldon on the set of the suspenseful, crime drama "Aren't You Surprised to See Me?", filmed in Dallas and telecast in February of 1962.

Martin Milner and George Maharis rehearse.

Sam Manners shares a lighter moment.

Directory of Photography Jack Marta relaxes between shots.

Paul Burke with Nancy Malone on the set of "Naked City" in the early 1960s. Malone later co-starred opposite Edmund O'Brien and Roy Thinnes in ABC's "The Long Hot Summer." Eventually she became a respected producer-director in network television and co-founded "Women in Film."

Nehemiah Persoff with John Wayne (and an unidentified newspaperman) on the set of "The Comancheros" in 1961. Persoff's portrayals on Route 66 as Divorovoi in "Incident on a Bridge," and as Jack in "First Class Mouliak" were memorable and illuminating.

Martin Milner with Signe Hasso and Jack Warden in "A Feat of Strength," which aired near the end of season two.

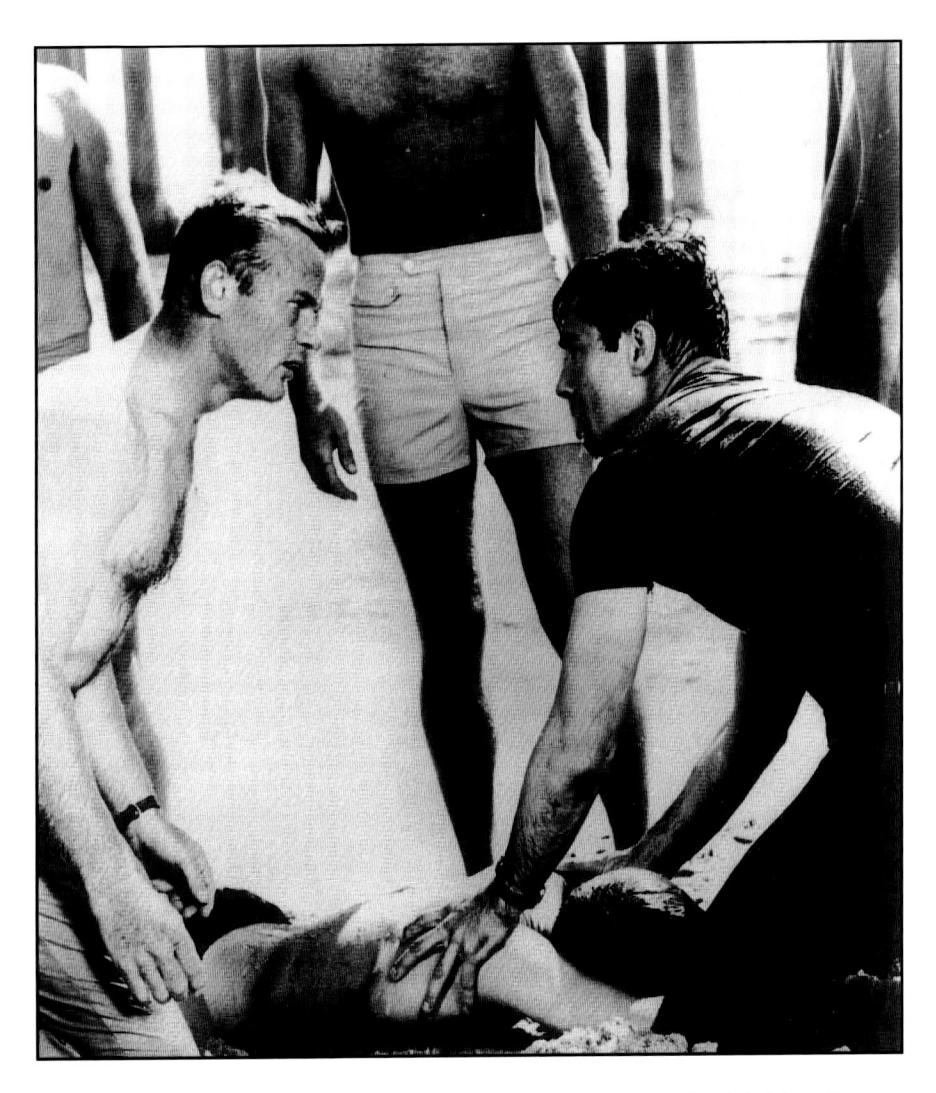

Tod (Martin Milner) convinces Buz (George Maharis) his efforts to revive surfer Jimmy Mills (Bruce Watson) are in vain in "Ever Ride the Waves in Oklahoma?," shown on October 12, 1962, during season three.

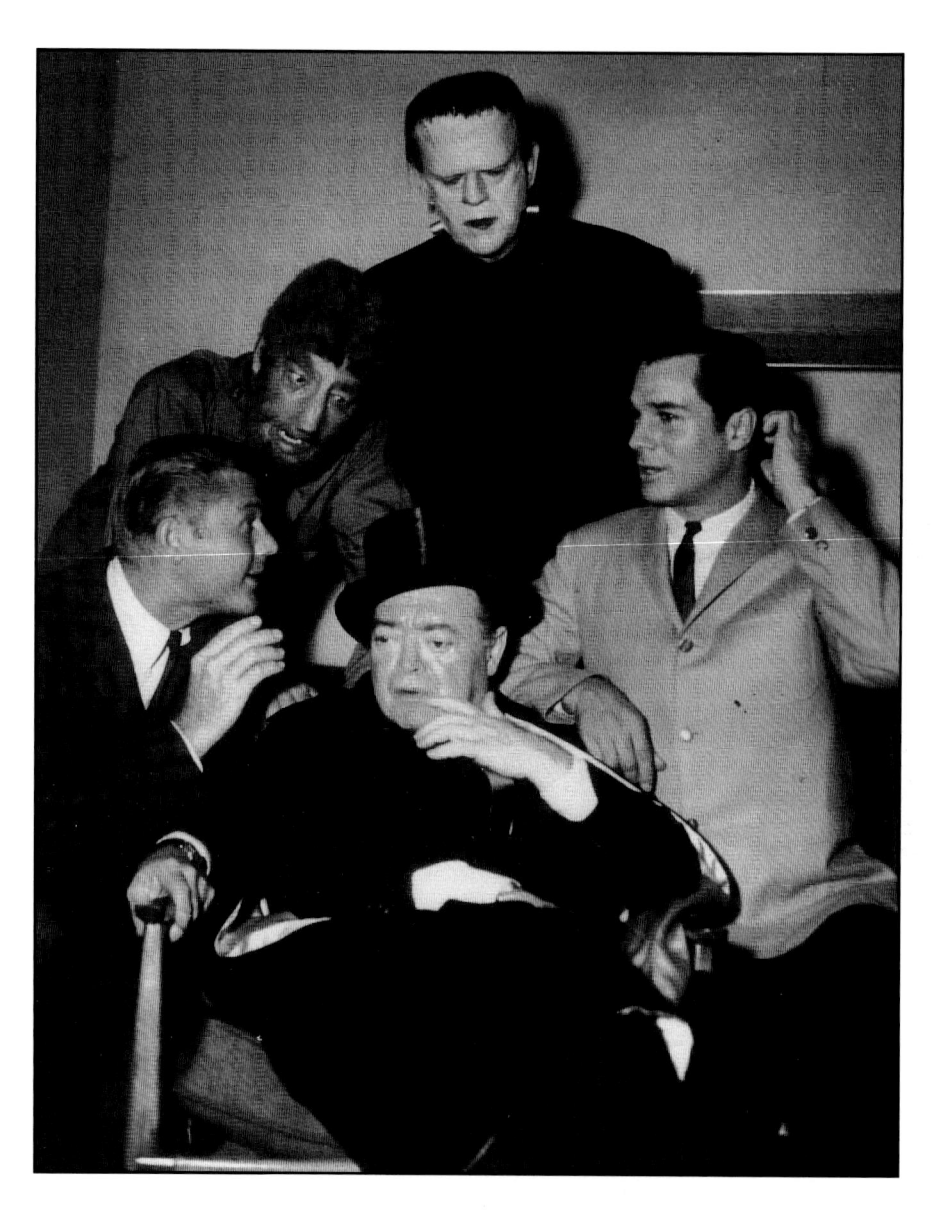

Milner and Maharis on the set of "Lizard's Leg and Owlet's Wing" with Boris Karloff (as the Frankenstein monster), Lon Chaney, Jr. (as the Wolfman), and Peter Lorre. The show was filmed at Chicago's O'Hare Inn and aired during the early part of season three. This was the only time Karloff ever appeared as the Frankenstein monster after starring in the three classic films of the 1930's.

After appearing in Otto Preminger's "Exodus" Maharis zoomed to TV stardom on "Route 66," and became the idol of millions. Charismatic, colorful, and dynamic as Buz, he proved to be irreplaceable.

Glenn Corbett with Martin Milner in 1963. Corbett appeared in nine episodes at the end of the third season and returned for the final year, portraying Linc Case, a troubled Vietnam veteran.

Mrs. Morgan Harper (Joan Crawford) seeks the aid of Linc Case (Glenn Corbett) when she learns that her husband plans to kill her in "Same Picture, Different Frame," the second episode of season four, shown in September of 1963.

The contrast between Milner and Maharis was unparalleled in 1960s network television, yet they displayed a unique chemistry which drew millions of viewers. Said Herbert Leonard, "If George had stayed, we would have run for years."

ROUTE 66 – FIRST SEASON

<u>Episode Titles</u>   <u>Air Dates</u>

1. Black November — 10/7/60
2. A Lance of Straw — 10/14/60
3. The Swan Bed — 10/21/60
4. The Man on the Monkey Board — 10/28/60
5. The Strengthening Angels — 11/4/60
6. Ten Drops of Water — 11/11/60
7. Three Sides — 11/18/60
8. Legacy for Lucia — 11/25/60
9. Layout at Glen Canyon — 12/2/60
10. The Beryllium Eater — 12/9/60
11. A Fury Slinging Flame — 12/30/60
12. Sheba — 1/6/61
13. The Quick and the Dead — 1/13/61
14. Play It Glissando — 1/20/61
15. The Clover Throne — 1/27/61
16. Fly Away Home (1) — 2/10/61
17. Fly Away Home (2) — 2/17/61
18. Sleep on Four Pillows — 2/24/61
19. An Absence of Tears — 3/3/61
20. Like a Motherless Child — 3/17/61
21. Effigy in Snow — 3/24/61
22. Eleven, the Hard Way — 4/7/61
23. Most Vanquished, Most Victorious — 4/14/61
24. Don't Count Stars — 4/28/61
25. The Newborn — 5/5/61
26. A Skill for Hunting — 5/12/61
27. Trap at Cordova — 5/26/61
28. The Opponent — 6/2/61
29. Welcome to Amity — 6/9/61
30. Incident on a Bridge — 6/16/61

#1. Black November

Produced by: **Herbert B. Leonard**
Written by: **Stirling Silliphant**
Directed by: **Philip Leacock**

When their car breaks down, Tod Stiles and Buz Murdock are stranded in the hostile lumber camp town of Garth. Aid is refused at every turn and only after a direct appeal to Caleb Garth, town tyrant, does the mechanic agree to fix their car. Local thugs attack Tod while he waits for repairs, and carry him off.

Buz, with the help of Jenny Slade, daughter of the general store's proprietor, finds out Tod has been taken to an abandoned prisoner-of-war camp on the outskirts of town. There, Buz and Jenny find Tod, and also discover Garth's son Paul placing flowers under a towering tree, the "wolf tree" that cuts light out from all other trees around. Dickson, the sheriff, sees them and reports to Garth. He goes to Jim Slade, the girl's father, and forces him to say Tod and Buz have assaulted the girl. Tod and Buz are threatened with lynching from the wolf tree.

Paul Garth prevents the hanging by telling his father that he and the town people were responsible for murdering a young German prisoner of war and the minister who was protecting him. The bodies were buried under the tree. Paul frees Tod and Buz and starts to chop down the wolf tree, symbol of the elder Garth's power.

Cast: Tod Stiles (*Martin Milner*), Buz Murdock (*George Maharis*), Caleb Garth (*Everett Sloane*), Jenny Slade (*Patty McCormack*), Slade (*Whit Bissell*), Dickson (*Robert Sorrells*), Clergyman (*House Jameson*), Paul (*Keir Dullea*).

#2. A Lance of Straw

Produced by: **Robert S. Bassler**
Written by: **Stirling Silliphant**
Directed by: **Roger Kay**

Tod and Buz drive to the gulf fishing village of Grand Isle, Louisiana to get jobs on a shrimp boat during the worst fishing season the natives have ever known. Beautiful Charlotte Duval hires them as crew for her trawler, the "Biloxi Queen." Charlotte, determined to follow in the footsteps of her father as a great fisherman, has consistently refused the marriage proposals of Jean Boussard, owner of the "Conquistador." Jean, extremely jealous, has beaten up any man Charlotte has hired. When Jean threatens Tod and Buz, Buz knocks him out. Andre Cabateau, the village elder, warns that Jean intends to make further trouble. Charlotte immediately puts to sea as a squall is building into a dangerous hurricane.

The "Conquistador" with Jean and his two-man crew follow. Charlotte, stops the "Biloxi Queen" at a small island to pray at her father's grave, then hauls a tremendous catch of shrimp aboard. As the trawler fights its way back through the hurricane, Buz hears a cry for help. The "Conquistador" has foundered. The "Biloxi Queen" saves Jean and his crew. Having proven her ability at sea, Charlotte realizes she loves Jean. Tod and Buz, with their share of the money from the great catch, drive away, leaving Charlotte and Jean together.

Cast: Tod (*Martin Milner*), Buz (*George Maharis*), Charlotte Duval (*Janice Rule*), Andre Cabateau (*Thomas Gomez*), Jean Boussard (*Nico Minardos*).

#3. The Swan Bed

Produced by: **Robert S. Bassler**
Written by: **Stirling Silliphant**
Directed by: **Elliot Silverstein**

Tod and Buz arrive in New Orleans as public health doctors are searching for the cause of an outbreak of parrot fever. They meet Carrie Purcell who lives with her mother in a shack near the Mississippi. Mrs. Purcell, a bitter woman living in her past, refuses to give Carrie money for a new dress to wear on a date with Tod and Buz. Carrie runs to her friend Amery Grant, caretaker of an old showboat beached in the mud. The showboat is being used by a gang headed by Bulloch as a storage house for parrots which they are smuggling into the country at enormous profit.

Carrie, after getting money for the dress, inadvertently finds a clue to the gang's operation. Two of Bulloch's hoods follow Carrie to gain possession of the clue. After Tod and Buz beat them off, Tod accompanies Carrie to the boat to get an explanation from Grant. Bulloch, gun in hand, locks them in a large room filled with birds carrying the infectious plague. Buz follows and hammers Bulloch into submission, thereby breaking up the smuggling ring. The public health authorities make plans to burn the plague-ridden showboat.

Cast: Tod (*Martin Milner*), Buz (*George Maharis*), Mrs. Purcell (*Betty Field*), Amery Grant (*Henry Hull*), Dr. Stafford (*Murray Hamilton*), Carrie (*Zina Bethune*), Bulloch (*Louis Zorich*), Randy Spring (*Elizabeth MacRae*), DeSavo (*Louis Guss*), Hercules George (*Jerome Raphel*).

#4. The Man on the Monkey Board

Executive Producer: **Herbert B. Leonard**
Written by: **Stirling Silliphant**
Directed by: **Roger Kay**

A helicopter carries Tod and Buz and Bartlett to their new jobs on an off-shore drilling barge in the Gulf of Mexico. Aboard the barge, both Tod and Buz become aware that Bartlett displays an unusual interest in the identities of his fellow workers. Then Buz saves Bartlett's life after an attempt is made to murder him. Bartlett realizes Tod and Buz are now in danger, since his unknown assailant must feel they are his friends. Bartlett tells Buz that he has been searching for the man responsible for the deaths of many innocent people in a concentration camp. He says that he has tracked him to the oil barge, and hopes to bring him to justice.

Bartlett's list of suspects dwindles to one man, Palmer. Bartlett gets absolute proof that Palmer is the mass murderer. With a gun in his pocket, Bartlett forces Palmer to accompany him to a helicopter, about to take off for the mainland. Palmer breaks away and clutches onto the pontoons of the aircraft as it rises in the sky. He is unable to attract the pilot's attention. Bartlett, Tod and Buz watch as the murderer falls to his death.

Cast: Tod (*Martin Milner*), Buz (*George Maharis*), Bartlett (*Lew Ayres*), Palmer (*Alfred Ryder*), Hanson (*Frank Overton*), Thompson (*Fred J. Scollay*), Jenkins (*Michael Conrad*), Albert (*Bruce Dern*).

#5. The Strengthening Angels

Executive Producer: **Herbert B. Leonard**
Written by: **Stirling Silliphant**
Directed by: **Arthur Hiller**

Tod and Buz give a lift to Lotti Montana who begs them to drive through the town of Sparrow Falls as quickly as possible. Lotti is recognized and the car is overtaken by Sheriff Hingle who takes the three of them to the City Jail. Tod and Buz are puzzled by Hingle's personal bitterness against Lotti until they learn that she killed his brother Al. Feeling that Lotti is being railroaded, Tod and Buz hire lawyer Richard Crown to defend her. Lotti, impressed by their friendship, tells them that Al broke into her home in a drunken state; while she was trying to fend him off, she killed him and ran away because she feared being lynched.

Buz learns that Lotti has a seven-year-old daughter, Teresa, being cared for by Daniel Wylie, a preacher, to whom Lotti went for refuge after the killing. Against Lotti's wishes, Buz questions Teresa who tells him there was another man standing outside the door on the night of the killing. After checking on the child's statement, Tod and Buz find that Crown was the second man. Crown corroborates Lotti's story. Hingle, learning the truth, reunites Lotti with her daughter as Tod and Buz ride away.

Cast: Tod (*Martin Milner*), Buz (*George Maharis*), Lotti Montana (*Suzanne Pleshette*), Daniel Wylie (*Harry Townes*), Hingle (*John Larch*), Crown (*Warren Stevens*).

#6. Ten Drops of Water

Produced by: **Robert S. Bassler**
Written by: **Howard Rodman**
Directed by: **Philip Leacock**

A short distance from Zion National Park, Vergil Page and his sister Helen are fighting a losing battle to hold onto the drought-ridden ranch their family has owned for over a hundred years. Proud, they refuse to ask for help. Helen reproaches Tod and Buz for returning her 12-year-old brother Homer's mule, since there is not enough water for the Pages or their cattle.

Tod and Buz use the motor of their car as a power plant to help the Pages deepen their well. Day and night, the struggle continues. As the cows begin to drop, Vergil, maddened by defeat, beats Homer's mule when it tries to get to the water in the tank. The mule runs off and Homer goes after him into a rising sandstorm.

Helen, Buz and Tod follow to rescue the boy. When the sandstorm subsides, they find him nestled close to his dead mule. Vergil asks his neighbors for aid and they flock from miles around to help the Pages get water. Their efforts are successful. However, as Tod and Buz drive away, Vergil finally gives in to Helen's pleas to sell the land so they can find an easier way of life.

Cast: Tod (*Martin Milner*), Buz (*George Maharis*), Vergil Page (*Burt Brinckerhoff*), Helen Page (*Deborah Walley*), Homer Page (*Tony Haig*), Mr. Pepperell (*Robert F. Simon*), Mrs. Pepperell (*Sara Haden*).

#7. Three Sides

Executive Producer: **Herbert B. Leonard**
Written by: **Stirling Silliphant**
Directed by: **Philip Leacock**

Curt and Karen Emerson, spoiled children of Gerald Emerson, a wealthy Oregon hop grower, seem determined to run their family name into the ground. Tod and Buz accept jobs from the elder Emerson, after Buz saves Curt from an unmerciful beating at the hands of Ted Becker, who has been forcing his attentions on Karen. Then Curt is responsible for the accidental death of Chuck Calloway, Emerson's loyal foreman. Tod and Buz fight a losing battle to save the crops after the workers, who feel Curt killed Calloway, leave. Emerson confesses to Tod and Buz that he has lost control over his children because he has tried to avoid the mistakes of his own tyrannical father.

Although Karen, her father, and Tod try to stop him, Curt leaves home. Karen, unable to win the help of her friends in harvesting her father's crop, turns to Becker. Becker, of course, senses an opportunity to get close to Karen. Both Curt and Buz learn that Karen has gone to see Becker. Curt gets there first. Becker starts for him with a boat hook. Buz breaks in and after a battering fight, knocks Becker unconscious. Buz and Tod drive away. Curt, Karen and Emerson, having finally found their mutual need for each other, start working together on the harvest.

Cast: Tod (*Martin Milner*), Buz (*George Maharis*), Gerald Emerson (*E. G. Marshall*), Karen (*Joey Heatherton*), Ted Becker (*Johnny Seven*), Curt Emerson (*Stephen Bolster*), Galloway (*Paul Genge*), Dr. Linton (*Phil Clarke*), Frank Palmer (*Tony Call*), Boy (*Bob Ament*), Station Man (*Dean Woolley*), Mrs. Hastings (*Winnie Coffin*).

#8. Legacy for Lucia

Executive Producer: **Herbert B. Leonard**
Teleplay by: **Stirling Silliphant**
Directed by: **Philip Leacock**

Working in an Oregon lumber mill, Tod and Buz meet Lucia Trapani who tells them she has come from Sicily to sell her only possession—the State of Oregon—for $7,800 in order to buy a new Madonna for her town's church. She shows Tod, Buz, and Bill Morrison, manager of the mill, a piece of cardboard on which Alec Hames, an American soldier with a great imagination, had willed her his claim to the timberland. After being given sanctuary by Lucia's family, Alec had been hunted down and killed by enemy soldiers. Morrison takes Lucia to see old Nathaniel Hobbs who raised Alec after the death of his parents. However, Nathaniel, who has become a hermit since Alec's death, refuses to see the girl, even though Morrison tells him that he has more than enough timberland to raise the money Lucia needs.

Tod and Buz are forced to tell her that Alec actually owned no property. As Lucia prepares to leave for home, Nathaniel comes to town. Shouting defiance, Nathaniel, finally touched by the girl's story, tells Buz to cut the trees. Tod, Buz and Morrison start chopping. Nathaniel himself takes charge of the operation and Lucia leaves for home with enough funds to buy the Madonna.

Cast: Tod (*Martin Milner*), Buz (*George Maharis*), Nathaniel (*Jay C. Flippen*), Morrison (*John Larch*), Lucia (*Arline Sax*), Secretary (*Vivi Janiss*).

#9 Layout at Glen Canyon

Executive Producer: **Herbert B. Leonard**
Written by: **Stirling Silliphant**
Directed by: **Elliot Silverstein**

Jeff Grady, head of the construction crew working at Glen Canyon Dam, Arizona, assigns Tod and Buz to act as bodyguards for a group of models chaperoned by Jo Galloway. They have come to take fashion shots at the dam. Learning of the girls presence, the construction workers try to storm their trailer campsite which has been posted out-of-bounds. Buz starts battling their leader, Lou Gillis. Jo breaks up the fight. Later, Eve Ellis tells Buz she left her husband when she found he had been seeing another woman.

After Betsy Carmel, another model, is responsible for an accident, Grady tells Jo to keep the girls away from his men. This leads to an argument. Jo tells Tod and Buz that she has been married to Grady; but had left him after their son died while his father was away on one of his never-ending construction assignments. Despite Grady's pleas, Jo still refuses his attempts for a reconciliation.

Then Tod and Buz discover Eve has run off with Lou Gillis. Fearing what may happen to Eve in her distraught state, Tod, Buz and Jo go after her. They find that Eve, having rebuffed Gillis' approaches, has wandered off into a dynamited area. Tod, Buz and Grady, risking their lives, make their way through the explosions and rescue Eve. Although Eve decides to forgive her repentant husband, Tod and Buz stand with Grady watching the plane carry Jo out of his life forever.

Cast: Tod (*Martin Milner*), Buz (*George Maharis*), Jeff Grady (*Charles McGraw*), Jo (*Bethel Leslie*), Eve (*Zohra Lampert*), Gillis (*Richard Shannon*), Nikko (*Fred Nakano*), Betsy (*Elizabeth MacRae*), Muriel (*Van Leslie*), Dana (*Donna Douglas*), Marvin (*William Benedict*).

#10. The Beryllium Eater

Executive Producer: **Herbert B. Leonard**
Written by: **Richard Collins**
Directed by: **Alvin Ganzer**

Shortly after Tod and Buz get jobs on the vast Utah mining properties of tycoon Fred Durant, Jack McConkie, an old prospector, finally hits a rich vein. When McConkie refuses to sell his claim to Durant, he is badly beaten by Babcock, Durant's top man, and two hirelings. Tod and Buz find McConkie in serious condition and take him to the mine's infirmary. McConkie is grateful to the boys and wills his properties to them in case he doesn't pull through, revealing the secret location.

Babcock takes Tod and Buz to Durant's luxurious home. They refuse Durant's offer to make the mining of McConkie's find a joint venture. Durant's wife, Wendy, who is attracted to Buz, asks him to drive her to town. She tells Buz she is sick of her husband's brutal methods and gets Tod and Buz the equipment needed to stake McConkie's claim from the motor pool at Durant's mine.

As Tod and Buz read McConkie's map to find the exact location of his find, they become aware that they are being watched from a distant point. After the boys set up false markers, Tod leaves to file claim. Babcock and his men surge in and overpower Buz. Tod returns and joins with Buz in a vicious fight to beat Babcock and his men, thereby making sure McConkie can work his claim in peace.

Cast: Tod (*Martin Milner*), Buz (*George Maharis*), Wendy (*Inger Stevens*), Durant (*Edward Binns*), Jack McConkie (*Edgar Buchanan*), Babcock (*Peter Mamakos*), Mine Doctor (*Freeman Lusk*).

#11. A Fury Slinging Flame

Executive Producer: **Herbert B. Leonard**
Written by: **Stirling Silliphant**
Directed by: **Elliot Silverstein**

Top scientist Mark Christopher, accompanied by his young son, Alan, and twenty followers, enters the caves at Carlsbad National Park where Tod and Buz are employed assisting tourists. Christopher refuses to obey Superintendent Jim Walsh's orders to return to the surface with his party since he feels that a thermonuclear attack is to be launched shortly. Tod meets Paula Shay, an aggressive newspaper woman who tries every scheme possible to get an exclusive story from Christopher. Christopher's ex-wife Frances comes to the caves with a court order and a U.S. Marshal to force Christopher to allow her to bring Alan to the surface.

When Christopher tells Frances that his belief that the blast will take place in ten minutes based on a series of code messages from Dr. Claridge, a friendly scientist, she derides them both as fools. Buz and Tod destroy the tape on Paula's miniature recorder after they learn she had sent for Frances as part of her scheme to get an exclusive story. All of the party, including Christopher, follow Frances when she takes Alan to the surface.

Cast: Tod (*Martin Milner*), Buz (*George Maharis*), Mark Christopher (*Leslie Nielsen*), Paula Shay (*Fay Spain*), Jim Walsh (*James Brown*), Dr. Claridge (*Conrad Nagel*), Frances Swanson (*Phyllis Hill*), Alan (*Jimmy Carter*).

#12. Sheba

Executive Producer: **Herbert B. Leonard**
Written by: **Stirling Silliphant**
Directed by: **William Claxton**

Laura Church is sent to prison, convicted of embezzling from her employer, the Western Cotton Oil Company in El Paso. At her trial, cattleman Woody Biggs denied her story that he lent her money, found in her possession, so she could pay the debts of her late husband who was employed in his stockyard. Later, Biggs wins Laura a parole, enabling her to return to work at the oil company. Tod and Buz engage Biggs in a vicious fight to save Laura from his advances, and she tells them that Biggs framed her to make her submit to his will.

Laura tells Buz she believes that Biggs started the stampede in the cattle pens in which her husband was killed. Going to the stockyard to learn the truth, Buz and Tod meet Hanna, Biggs' longtime cashier whom he has just cast aside. A fight breaks out between Biggs and Buz, during which Buz forces Biggs into the huge cattle pen where Laura's husband was killed. In response to Buz's shouts, Hanna blows a cattle horn, starting a stampede. To save his life, Biggs admits his guilt. Tod crashes through the fence in a pickup truck and rescues both men.

Cast: Tod (*Martin Milner*), Buz (*George Maharis*), Woody Biggs (*Lee Marvin*), Laura Church (*Whitney Blake*), Pedro Regal (*Rico Alaniz*), Bartender (*Stuart Nisbet*), Johnny Langway (*Raymond Guth*), Prison Matron (*Doris Karnes*), Hanna Martin (*Carol Ohmart*).

#13. The Quick and the Dead

Executive Producer: **Herbert B. Leonard**
Teleplay by: **Stirling Silliphant**
Directed by: **Alvin Ganzer**

Tod enters the stock-car racing event in the Grand Prix at Riverside, California. Beatrice Webster, second wife of Cord Webster, a race car driver, watches Tod's warm-up spin and feels he can solve her problem. Bea, fearing for her husband's life, is trying to make him quit racing. She is violently opposed by Katherine Webster, her stepdaughter, who feels her dad is still tops on the track. Bea persuades Tod to drive Webster's racer in the main event. After watching Tod in a trial run, Cord accepts his wife's decision. Tod meets Katy, falls for her and is torn by the conflicting stories of Bea and Katy. Cord, however, agrees to give up racing after Bea threatens to leave him. Katy knows she must work fast. She persuades Tod to drive to Mexico and, knowing how much he has fallen for her, adds she will marry him there if he wishes it.

Buz realizes Tod is being used. Backed by Jeff Russell, Cord's mechanic, he gets Tod to see that Katy will do anything to keep him out of town on the day of the race. Tod enters the race in Webster's car against the field's top drivers. The car catches on fire. Tod, wavering, staggers from the car, his overalls smoking. Buz throws a drop-cloth around Tod, saving him from any possible injury. On the basis of laps completed, Tod takes third place. Shortly after, Tod and Buz return to the open road.

Cast: Tod (*Martin Milner*), Buz (*George Maharis*), Jeff (*Regis Toomey*), Doty (*Pamela Searle*), Bea (*Betsy Jones Moreland*), Len (*Harvey Korman*), Katy (*Susan Kohner*), Cord (*Frank Overton*).

#14. Play It Glissando

Executive Producer: **Herbert B. Leonard**
Written by: **Stirling Silliphant**
Directed by: **Lewis Allen**

On California's Pacific Coast, Tod and Buz join singer Kitty Parker at a performance by trumpeter Gabe Johnson and his combo. Driving back, Tod swerves out of the path of another car that smashes into a post. The driver is Jana Johnson, Gabe's wife. She claims that Gabe, driven by insane jealousy, has tried to kill her. At the sheriff's office, Jana phones her wealthy mother in Southampton, but gets no answer. Gabe arrives and convinces everyone that Jana's claims are untrue. However, Buz and Tod take Jana under their wing and the terrified girl sits up all night clasping a small automatic. She tells them she wants to be free of the man who is constantly trying to climb out of the world on the rungs of his golden trumpet notes.

After Jana promises to join them, Tod and Buz leave for breakfast with Kitty. Gabe arrives. He and Jana have almost effected a reconciliation when Jana receives a phone call from her mother's lawyer. She learns that Gabe has concealed the fact that her mother has been dead for two months. She grabs her automatic and forces him to leave. As Tod and Buz are driving Jana to meet her mother's lawyer, Gabe tries to shoot her. He hits Tod. Tod is taken to the hospital. Gabe escapes. Buz and Jana join the search for him. After one dangerous brush with Gabe, they finally find him playing his trumpet on an auditorium's empty stage. Jana rushes to Gabe's arms once more. Later, waiting for Tod to recover, Buz realizes Jana will stand by Gabe no matter what happens.

Cast: Tod (*Martin Milner*), Buz (*George Maharis*), Jana Johnson (*Ann Francis*), Gabe Johnson (*Jack Lord*), Kitty (*Barbara Bostock*), Lieut. Mangano (*Harold J. Stone*).

#15. The Clover Throne

Executive Producer: **Herbert B. Leonard**
Written by: **Herman Meadow**
Directed by: **Arthur Hiller**

In California, Tod and Buz find jobs in Adam Darcey's date fields. Adam's legs are paralyzed. Sitting on his porch, his rifle next to him, Adam has two problems. One, he loves his beautiful ward, Sweet Thing, who is constantly searching for the money she believes he has hidden and which she hopes will help her get away from him. His other problem is to stop the construction of a road across his property. Adam has fenced in a tractor left by the construction crew; he refuses to give it up until guaranteed the road will not cross his land. Sweet Thing has been flirting with Joe Goss, a member of a prison road gang, to help her get Adam's money. When Sweet Thing makes the same play for Buz, Goss' jealousy is aroused. He attacks Sweet Thing. Buz rushes to her aid and after a terrific fight, beats Goss.

Meanwhile, a huge bulldozer has been driven up to the tractor and starts pulling it away. Hobbling on his crutches, Adam makes his way to the tractor, catches onto it, but is dragged along behind. Tod and Buz rescue Adam, and construction of the road across Adam's property is called off. Adam confesses he pretended he couldn't walk because he thought this would keep Sweet Thing at his side. Although Adam offers her the money she has always wanted, Sweet Thing realizes she loves Adam and the two walk together to their new-found happiness.

Cast: Tod (*Martin Milner*), Buz (*George Maharis*), Adam (*Jack Warden*), Sweet Thing (*Anne Helm*), Joe Goss (*Arthur Batanides*).

#16. Fly Away Home
(Part 1)

Executive Producer: **Herbert B. Leonard**
Written by: **Stirling Silliphant**
Directed by: **Arthur Hiller**

Tod and Buz head for the Windus Dusting Co., near Phoenix, Arizona. Tod was taught to fly by Jack Windus, and now hopes to serve an apprenticeship which will lead to his becoming a crop duster. Tod doesn't know that Windus was killed in a crash. His widow, Dora Windus, trying to carry on the company, refuses to accept her husband's death and believes he will return. The mainstay in the operation is veteran pilot Summers. Summers believes he is a jinx, since everyone who has ever been associated with him in flying has been killed. Summers has moved from job to job, trying to escape his wife Christina. Christina is singing at a Phoenix nightclub to be near him. Buz hears her sing and falls for her.

Dora's daughter Vicki, infuriated by her mother's refusal to accept her husband's death, claims Summers killed her father. Dora has earned an unenviable reputation for herself throughout the area. Meanwhile, Dora tries desperately to win new business for the failing outfit. Summers, feeling his jinx will attach itself to Tod, refuses to teach him. By the time Dora gets a job to tide them over, Summers has gone on a drinking spree during which he tells Christina to get out of his life. Unable to find Summers, Dora tells Tod he can have a job at the company if he and Buz find Summers, which they do. Although Summers tells Tod he is too young to die, he finally accepts him as an apprentice.

Cast: Tod (*Martin Milner*), Buz (*George Maharis*), Summers (*Michael Rennie*), Christina (*Dorothy Malone*), Dora (*Cathy Lewis*), Vicki (*Jenny Maxwell*).

#17. Fly Away Home (Part 2)

Executive Producer: **Herbert B. Leonard**
Written by: **Stirling Silliphant**
Directed by: **Arthur Hiller**

Summers starts training Tod to be a crop duster. Russell, a planter, realizes that Dora is desperately in need of money. He offers her the job of spraying his acreage, but insists that sulfur be used. Dora knows how deadly sulfur is and refuses Russell's offer, although she knows the job is vital to her company's survival.

Dora tells Vicki she will have to close down the operation unless she gets some new contracts. Vicki is jubilant. She tells her mother everyone thinks she is crazy, since they believe she is pretending her husband is still alive. Vicki blames Summers for her father's death, then tells her mother that she can only be her daughter again, when she finally admits her husband is dead and shows some of the normal emotions she has never displayed. Dora reaffirms her belief that her husband will return.

While teaching Tod, Summers learns Dora is closing the field. He orders his plane's hoppers to be filled with sulfur and accepts the Russell job. Flying over the Russell acreage, the plane ignites and flames envelope it. There is no fear in Summers' face, rather a quiet acceptance of the inevitable as he crashes. Dora now acknowledges her husband's death. Vicki and her mother are reunited. They decide to run the company together. Christina realizes her long quest is over. Although Buz reaffirms his love for her, Christina leaves to lose herself in a new and lonely world.

Cast: Tod (*Martin Milner*), Buz (*George Maharis*), Summers (*Michael Rennie*), Christina (*Dorothy Malone*), Dora (*Cathy Lewis*), Vicki (*Jenny Maxwell*), Russell (*Ford Rainey*).

#18. Sleep on Four Pillows

Executive Producer: **Herbert B. Leonard**
Written by: **Stirling Silliphant**
Directed by: **Ted Post**

In Los Angeles, after finding residence in a men's club, Buz goes to work as a door-to-door salesman, while Tod takes a course at UCLA. They run into Jan who informs them her suitcase and purse have been stolen, and that she is being trailed by a mob bent on killing her father, a former underworld leader. The boys are skeptical about her wild story and drop her off with $20. Meanwhile, a nationwide search has been started for Jan by her mother, State Congresswoman Marva Ansel-Emerson, whose husband, a wealthy contractor, is in Brazil. Baer, head of a detective agency, has also been engaged for the search. Jan, disguising herself in men's clothes, breaks into the boys' room and again pleads for their help.

Jan, who has been leaving clues to make her mother believe she is being held for ransom, drops a message on one of Buz's sales slips. Baer and his aide find Buz. When they try to get to Jan, Buz finally believes her story about being pursued, and knocks out both men. Jan calls her mother and arranges a meeting in a UCLA building. Marva asks Jan about the ransom money. Jan says she ran away hoping to win her parents' affection which she feels she has never had. The Emersons take Jan on a trip to South America. Tod and Buz are given the use of their luxurious home and pool until they return.

Cast: Tod (*Martin Milner*), Buz (*George Maharis*), Jan (*Patty McCormack*), Baer (*Larry Gates*), Marva (*Marianne Stewart*), Police Lieutenant (*John Beradino*).

#19. An Absence of Tears

Produced by: **Herbert B. Leonard**
Written by: **Stirling Silliphant**
Directed by: **Alvin Ganzer**

Blinky Ober, a mobster, and two underlings, Poke and Chico, drive up to a gas station. Shortly after, Jeff Stevens and his blind wife Donna stop there. Jeff stays in the car, while Donna is led to a phone booth by Rex, her seeing eye dog. The attendant sees Poke toying with the cash register, and draws his gun. Poke shoots him and then kills Jeff. Donna makes her way to Jeff's dead body. Donna tells Lieut. Julian Cobb that she knows the men by their voices, and is going to kill them with the same model gun they used on Jeff. Donna returns to her job as instructor in a dance studio. Tod, who has received 20 dance lessons as a birthday gift, meets her. Later, Tod buys the gun for her. Then Donna calls on Rudy Lang, a top mobster. She agrees to a romantic attachment if he finds the men who killed Jeff.

Donna receives a phone call from Lang. Tod and Buz trail her to his place. After giving Donna the information, Lang tries to hold her to their bargain. Tod and Buz arrive. While Buz pounds Lang to a pulp, Donna leaves and breaks into the mob's waterfront shack. Guided by Rex, she memorizes the location of every object in the room. When Ober and Poke return, she tells them she is going to kill them. However, while holding a gun, she realizes she is unable to use it to gain revenge. While she hesitates, Chico enters and smashes the gun from her hands. Buz and Tod arrive and rescue her from the mobsters.

Cast: Tod (*Martin Milner*), Buz (*George Maharis*), Donna (*Martha Hyer*), Rex (*Rin Tin Tin*), Poke (*Herb Armstrong*), Blinky (*Joseph Ruskin*), Midge (*Mary Webster*), Lt. Cobb (*Herman Rudin*), Cab Driver (*Lewis Charles*), Chico (*Joe Abdullah*), Rudy (*Paul Richards*).

First Season 53

#20. Like a Motherless Child

Produced by: **Herbert B. Leonard**
Written by: **Howard Rodman**
Directed by: **David Lowell Rich**

Tod and Buz pick up Martin, a 10-year-old fugitive from an orphanage. Tod decides to take the boy back. Buz's own experience as an orphan has caused him to identify with Martin. Upset with Tod, Buz leaves and gets a job in Fallon, where the annual livestock auction is about to start. Buz rents a trailer next to one occupied by Hannah Ellis. Hannah is in charge of Jake Hunter's girls, a group of hoofers who shill for carnival gambling concessions. Jake, an ex-hoofer, is brutal in his treatment of Hannah and the girls. Hannah's own son, who would now be Buz's age, was taken from her by an adoption agency when he was an infant. She is immediately drawn to Buz. Tod follows Buz to the trailer camp. Despite their differences of opinion, there is still a bond between them.

Tod realizes that Buz has become emotionally involved with Hannah. When every attempt to stop Buz from seeing Hannah fails, Tod asks Buz to do him one last favor. Buz agrees to accompany Tod to a roadhouse. There, Hannah and the girls are shilling for the bar and gambling tables. Buz is deeply moved by Hannah's humiliation at being discovered. Angered by what Tod has done, Buz engages him in a fight. They go at it until both are breathless. Buz realizes Tod is right and leaves town with him. Jake finally feels a touch of compassion for Hannah, and they are brought together for the first time. Before leaving with Tod, Buz is pleased to find that Martin has found happiness at the orphanage.

Cast: Tod (*Martin Milner*), Buz (*George Maharis*), Hannah (*Sylvia Sidney*), Jake (*Jack Weston*), Liz (*Nina Vaughn*), Peg (*Joyce Horne*), Theresa (*Chris Carter*), Frieda (*Barbara Hines*), Chuck (*Rodney Bell*), Alley (*Ben Johnson*), Martin (*Brad Herrman*).

#21. Effigy in Snow

Produced by: **Herbert B. Leonard**
Written by: **Stirling Silliphant**
Directed by: **Alvin Ganzer**

A short time after Tod and Buz find employment at a Squaw Village ski lodge, Armand Fontaine murders Shirley Hughes on a snowy slope. As a child, Armand had been present when his father discovered his wife with another man. Although the elder Fontaine left home immediately with his son, Armand's mind cracked under the impact of the scene; he erroneously believes his father killed his unfaithful wife. Since then, Armand has looked to find a woman to match the purity projected by his mother's wedding picture. For a while he thought Shirley was this woman. When Shirley betrayed an all-too-human flaw, Armand, acting out the fantastic picture in his mind, killed her. Returning to the lodge before Shirley's body has been discovered, Armand is attracted to Penny Foster, a young widow. Buz assists Penny in running the ski shop.

Penny's actions destroy Armand's initial image of her. He invites her to ski with him. After they leave, Shirley's body is found, and Armand's father arrives to catch his son before he gives way to his murderous compulsion. While skiing, Penny realizes Armand is trying to kill her and tries to escape. Meanwhile, Tod and Buz have joined a search party to rescue Penny. Armand skis to a U.S. Forest Service cannon used to keep masses of snow from becoming dangerous avalanches. He opens fire on his pursuers. However, the elder Fontaine makes his way to his son. Armand breaks completely. Tod and Buz arrive to find Armand clinging to his father for sanctuary.

Cast: Tod (*Martin Milner*), Buz (*George Maharis*), Armand (*Scott Marlowe*), Penny (*Jeanne Bal*), Mr. Fontaine (*George Macready*), Otto (*Kurt Kreuger*).

#22. Eleven, The Hard Way

Produced by: **Herbert B. Leonard**
Written by: **George Clayton Johnson**
Directed by: **William A. Graham**

Broken Knee, Nevada appears to be on the verge of becoming a ghost town, with the closing of its silver mine. Although Mr. Oliver, the ultra-conservative paymaster, tells them it is insanity, the citizens of the town gather their life savings and turn the money over to Sam Keep, a proprietor of the local pool parlor, who has a reputation of being a successful gambler. They feel Sam can go to Reno and run the stake up into enough to turn the town into an attractive tourist spot. Oliver decides to accompany Sam to Reno. As he is about to leave, Sam is attacked by four muggers who have discovered he has the money. Tod and Buz, who have just arrived, beat them off and save the money. Oliver hires Tod and Buz to follow Sam and himself to Reno and keep an eye on Sam.

Sam Looks as if he is going to break the table, but finally loses all the money. Tod and Buz feel Sam can make a comeback and they chip in everything they have. Sam admits to Buz he never was a successful gambler; he just made up stories about his winnings. When Sam says they need someone new to shoot for them, Buz thinks of Oliver, an expert with figures. Although Oliver doesn't know anything about the game, Tod, Buz and Sam teach him. Playing for the first time, Oliver wins a large sum of money. Then "gambling fever" gets him. Although he starts to lose, he continues to play. Sam finally forces him to leave with his winnings. With more than enough money, Sam and Oliver, accompanied by Tod and Buz, prepare to leave for Broken Knee to put the town back on the map.

Cast: Tod (*Martin Milner*), Buz (*George Maharis*), Sam Keep (*Walter Matthau*), Francis Oliver (*Edward Andrews*), Monty Knight (*Guy Raymond*), Dora Knight (*Debbie Megowan*).

#23. Most Vanquished, Most Victorious

Produced by: **Herbert B. Leonard**
Written by: **Stirling Silliphant**
Directed by: **William D. Faralla**

A letter from Tod's Aunt Kitty brings Tod and Buz to a slum area in Los Angeles. Kitty had broken with her family when she ran away with a man at the age of 19. Now Kitty is dying in a poverty-stricken neighborhood, frequented by a gang headed by Cazador. Kitty pleads with Tod to find her daughter Carole, and he promises to do so. Although Carole has made a wonderful impression, no one seems to know where she has gone. The search leads them to Timmy's, an underworld dive in Gardena. Alice, a hostess, tells them Carole disappeared months before, after meeting Juan Domingo, a young artist, who also lives in the slum area near Kitty. Juan tells Tod and Buz that Carole had posed for a series of photos which he hoped would take Carole and himself out of their unhappy environment.

Juan tells Tod and Buz that Cazador and his gang, searching for new thrills, had broken in while Carole was posing. They threatened to destroy all Juan's paintings unless Carole danced for them. Carole had agreed, but while trying to escape their brutality, had fallen on a knife and died. Tod and Buz return to Cazador's hangout. In a vicious fight, Tod and Buz beat Cazador and his mob. Tod and Buz return to Kitty. Kitty dies finally aware of what a wonderful person her daughter was.

Cast: Tod (*Martin Milner*), Buz (*George Maharis*), Kitty Chamberlain (*Beatrice Straight*), Dr. Clemente (*Royal Dano*), Cazador (*Pat DeSimone*), Davey Briggs (*Frank de Kova*), Alice (*Elizabeth Allen*), Juan Domingo (*John Alonze*).

#24. Don't Count Stars

Produced by: **Herbert B. Leonard**
Written by: **Stirling Silliphant**
Directed by: **Paul Wendkos**

Buz and Tod save Mike McKay from drowning. Alcoholic and impractical, Mike is the guardian of his 9-year-old niece Linda McKay. Linda's parents, who died in an accident, willed her the Sands Motel. Frank Hammond, trustee and executor of Linda's estate, feels that Mike is a bad influence for the young girl, and that the long list of bad accounts run up by Mike's racetrack friends will eventually bankrupt her estate. Hammond announces that a petition requesting the removal of Mike as Linda's guardian will be heard before Judge Lindstrom in two days. Mike, ashamed of his actions and afraid to face the court, tries to run away. Linda, who loves her uncle, engages Tod and Buz to keep Mike at his motel and in a sober state during that time.

Buz keeps Mike prisoner in his room, sometimes using physical restraint to do so. Tod and Linda collect the back debts from the gambling clientele. Mike breaks down and tells Buz that he actually is Linda's father; that after the death of his wife, shortly after Linda was born, he felt the infant would have a better chance if adopted by his childless brother and sister-in-law. Buz finally gets Mike to realize that Linda needs his love more than anything else. Linda is overjoyed when Mike announces his intentions of staying with her. Father and daughter leave for the hearing, and a happy and new life together.

Cast: Tod (*Martin Milner*), Buz (*George Maharis*), Mike McKay (*Dan Duryea*), Linda McKay (*Susan Melvin*), Frank Hammond (*Vaughn Taylor*), Ernie Bassard (*Oliver McGowan*).

#25. The Newborn

Produced by: **Herbert B. Leonard**
Written by: **Stirling Silliphant**
Directed by: **Arthur Hiller**

In New Mexico, Tod and Buz get jobs on a ranch owned by ruthless Frank Ivy. Ivy's reckless son seduced an Indian girl named Kawna; Ivy had forced him to marry the girl. Later, his son, in a drunken state, was accidentally killed. Now Kawna is pregnant. Although she prays to die, Kawna has gone to an adobe hut to give birth. Ivy, Roman (his henchman), and Buz go to bring Kawna back to the ranch, where Ivy insists his grandchild should be born. Buz, angered by Ivy and Roman's treatment of the girl, interferes, but Ivy knocks him out from behind with the butt of a gun.

After Kawna is brought to the ranch, Tod and Buz prepare to leave. They find Kawna, who has escaped from the house, hiding on the floor of their car. Roman forces them into a fight before they can go. Tod and Buz knock him out and drive away with Kawna. Ivy, finding Kawna has fled, starts his men in pursuit of her. Tod and Buz get Kawna to a deserted village where Kawna's baby is born. Kawna dies after giving birth.

Tod and Buz fight their way through Ivy's encircling men. Roman tries to stop them, but is killed when he falls on an embedded pick. Tod and Buz take the infant to Father Prior and Kawna's tribe. Ivy arrives with his men and demands the infant be given to him. However, when Father Prior refers to the mistakes Ivy made in bringing up his own son, Ivy feels beaten. Tod and Buz stand with Father Prior and the Indians who are holding the infant as Ivy and his men ride away.

Cast: Tod (*Martin Milner*), Buz (*George Maharis*), Frank Ivy (*Albert Dekker*), Kawna (*Arline Sax*), Roman (*Robert Duvall*), Father Prior (*Denver Pyle*), Satterfield (*Bing Russell*).

#26. A Skill for Hunting

Produced by: **Herbert B. Leonard**
Written by: **Jack Turley and M. Gelman**
Directed by: **David Lowell Rich**

Tod stops Bob "Hump" Humphrey, vice president of a trucking combine from shooting a doe on a wildlife refuge in New Mexico. Hump shoots the back tires of Tod's car. Tod and Buz follow Hump to Santa Fe where a convention of his truckers is in progress. Gus Patton, Hump's partner, becomes infuriated on learning that Hump is trying to run a small trucker out of business. He tells Hump that he is going to take advantage of a clause in their partnership which will force Hump to sell his share. Tod and Buz arrive. Trinket, Hump's girlfriend, tries to get them to leave but Buz beats Hump in a rough-and-tumble brawl. Hump warns Buz and Tod that he will get even.

Tod and Buz are arrested by Fred Capper, a game warden, and find that Hump had framed them for shooting the doe. They are taken to the local jail. Trinket pays their fine and gets them out of jail. Meanwhile, Hump, claiming satisfaction with the sale of his company, persuades Gus to go hunting with him. Determined to prove their innocence by forcing Hump to testify, Tod and Buz trail him to the hunting lodge. Trinket follows the boys. Hump tricks Gus onto the ledge of the precipice. When Gus refuses a last appeal to continue the partnership, Hump pushes him off the precipice. Realizing that Buz, Tod and Trinket have seen his murderous act, Hump pursues them, determined to wipe out every witness. Buz finds an animal trap and sets it in Hump's path. As Hump approaches for the kill, the trap snaps, and he realizes his ruthless career has ended.

Cast: Tod (*Martin Milner*), Buz (*George Maharis*), Hump (*Gene Evans*), Trinket (*Joanna Moore*), Gus (*Harold J. Stone*), Frank (*Paul Genge*), Fred Capper (*Warren Kemmerling*).

#27. Trap at Cordova

Produced by: **Leonard Freeman**
Teleplay by: **Stirling Silliphant**
Directed by: **Arthur Hiller**

In New Mexico Miguel Delgado cleverly traps Tod and Buz into coming with him to the secluded town of Cordova. Tod and Buz are completely baffled by Delgado's motives when he tells them they have broken the law and must spend a year in the town. Delgado, who is trying to keep the community's way of life, has refused to send the town's children on the three-hour-a-day trip to the district school. Having learned that Tod graduated from college, Delgado tells him that he must spend the year teaching upper grades, while Buz teaches the primary grades. A group of young men stop Tod and Buz from leaving. Little by little Tod and Buz are won over to Delgado's plan to educate the town's children.

Delgado manages to parry every thrust of the sheriff to get the children to the district school. Finally the sheriff threatens to arrest Delgado, Tod and Buz. Delgado's daughter, Anita, who does not share her father's way of thinking, pleads with Tod and Buz to leave, but they stand by Delgado. News of the affair reaches the state capitol. Senator Chaves invites Tod to address the New Mexican legislature and express his viewpoint. In an impassioned speech, Tod pleads with the legislators to allow the humble people to live their own way of life. Before Tod and Buz leave Cordova, the town is given a teacher and a playground for its children.

Cast: Tod (*Martin Milner*), Buz (*George Maharis*), Miguel Delgado (*Thomas Gomez*), Anita Delgado (*Dianne Foster*), Sheriff Canfield (*James Brown*).

#28. The Opponent

Produced by: **Leonard Freeman**
Written by: **Stirling Silliphant**
Directed by: **David Lowell Rich**

Tod and Buz detour into Youngstown, Ohio to see Buz's boyhood friend, fighter Johnny Copa, battle Otto Zempski. Buz hasn't seen Johnny in years and remembers him as a promising young fighter. Although Tod cautions him that Johnny might have changed, Buz bets Poochy and Mace $135 that Johnny will beat Zempski.

Tod and Buz track Johnny to a fourth-rate hotel. Scully, Johnny's trainer, tells them that Johnny is a worn-out fighter, and he is being used as a punching bag for up-and-coming hopefuls. Susan, Johnny's girlfriend, is trying to get him to quit the ring. Buz feels that Johnny, with his confidence restored by one victory, can be convinced to give up the ring.

Although Scully tells him to stop dreaming, Buz persuades the trainer to allow him to work in Johnny's corner on the night of the fight. Spurred on by Buz, Johnny beats Zempski after a grueling battle. Both Tod and Buz are disgusted when Johnny expresses his belief that he is ready for the big time once more. Susan threatens to leave Johnny. Tod and Buz watch Johnny and Susan go to the depot and board the next bus leaving for Susan's home.

Cast: Tod (*Martin Milner*), Buz (*George Maharis*), Johnny Copa (*Darren McGavin*), Susan (*Lois Nettleton*), Scully (*Edward Asner*), Poochy (*Clement Fowler*), Mace (*David C. Clarke*), Gym Owner (*Al Lewis*), Anson (*Ben Yaffee*), Otto (*Joseph Archer*).

#29. Welcome to Amity

Produced by: **Leonard Freeman**
Written by: **Will Lorin**
Directed by: **Arthur Hiller**

Tod and Buz can't understand why the inhabitants of Amity have joined together against Joan Maslow. After a long absence, Joan drives into town with a two-wheel trailer attached to her car. Tod and Buz learn that Joan has purchased a plot in the cemetery on the hill. She is determined to remove her mother's body from an unmarked grave in the town's Potter's Field to the cemetery on the hill. She is carrying a headstone for her mother in the trailer.

Tod and Buz are unable to find anyone in town willing to help Joan. They finally agree to assist the distraught girl themselves. Every obstacle is placed in their path, and they are finally stopped when Joan's aunt, Mrs. Watson, legally contests the re-burial. Pressed by Tod and Buz for a reason, Mrs. Watson tells them that Joan's mother was a monster whose immoral actions had all but corrupted and demoralized the town; that she had died in an accident while in a drunken state.

Joan surprises Mrs. Watson, Tod and Buz when she tells them she knew all these things and that she hated her mother. However, Joan adds that she feels the only way she can erase the nightmare of her mother's existence which haunts her dreams is to give her a decent burial. Tod and Buz leave Joan who has finally found peace of mind.

Cast: Tod (*Martin Milner*), Buz (*George Maharis*), Mrs. Watson (*Martha Scott*), Joan Maslow (*Susan Oliver*).

#30. Incident on a Bridge

Produced by: **Leonard Freeman**
Written by: **Stirling Silliphant**
Directed by: **David Lowell Rich**

In Cleveland, beneath an overhead bridge by the river, amidst intense police activity, Tod and Buz recount their involvement in a bizarre set of circumstances. It begins in a sand and gravel yard near the Russian-American section of town where they witness a bully named Orlov strangling a helpless worker named Divorovoi (an ugly and Neanderthal-type man). The reason: Divorovoi is accused of harassing Anna, the beautiful speech-impaired daughter of his boss Volovich who has promised her hand in marriage to Orlov. When Buz intervenes, Orlov attacks him. While they struggle, Tod rescues Divorovoi and prevents him from killing Orlov in retaliation.

Volovich fires Divorovoi and hires Tod and Buz who room and board at his house. When Orlov later accosts Anna in a jealous rage, Divorovoi breaks his neck and flees. At Orlov's wake, Anna is taken by a desperate Divorovoi who is aware of Volovich's inhuman treatment. Divorovoi professes his unselfish love for her in a way she has never known from her cruel and tyrannical father. However, with a dim, uncertain future, and nothing to offer her, Divorovoi bids Anna farewell and flees.

Anna follows him with the police in pursuit. Tod and Buz hear shots and see Divorovoi in flight, pursued by Anna. At the bridge, Anna catches up to Divorovoi. The look in her eye conveys her future is with him however uncertain it may be. They climb to the catwalk of the railroad bridge together. Tod and Buz get close and attempt to reach them before the police do but are cut off by a passing train, unable to

#30. Incident on a Bridge (Cont'd)

see if the couple jumped onto the passing freight train or missed and drowned in the river. Tod and Buz are left to wonder what happened to Divorovoi and Anna who truly found a reality of oneness before they disappeared from view.

Cast: Tod (*Martin Milner*), Buz (*George Maharis*), Divorovoi (*Nehemiah Persoff*), Anna (*Lois Smith*), Volovich (*Muni Seroff*), Orlov (*Allen Melvin*), Hodges (*Herb Voland*).

ROUTE 66 – SECOND SEASON

Episode Title	Air Date
31. A Month of Sundays	9/22/61
32. Blue Murder	9/29/61
33. Good Night, Sweet Blues	10/6/61
34. Birdcage on My Foot	10/13/61
35. First Class Mouliak	10/20/61
36. Once to Every Man	10/27/61
37. The Mud Nest	11/10/61
38. A Bridge Across Five Days	11/17/61
39. Mon Petit Chou	11/24/61
40. Some of the People, Some of the Time	12/1/61
41. The Thin White Line	12/8/61
42. And the Cat Jumped Over the Moon	12/15/61
43. Burning for Burning	12/29/61
44. To Walk with the Serpent	1/5/62
45. A Long Piece of Mischief	1/19/62
46. 1800 Days to Justice	1/26/62
47. City of Wheels	2/2/62
48. How Much a Pound is Albatross?	2/9/62
49. Aren't You Surprised to See Me?	2/16/62
50. You Never Had It So Good	2/23/62
51. Shoulder the Sky, My Lad	3/2/62
52. Blues for a Left Foot	3/9/62
53. Go Read the River	3/16/62
54. Even Stones Have Eyes	3/30/62
55. Love is a Skinny Kid	4/6/62
56. Kiss the Maiden All Forlorn	4/13/62
57. Two on the House	4/20/62
58. There I Am, There I Always Am	5/4/62
59. Between Hello and Goodbye	5/11/62
60. A Feat of Strength	5/18/62
61. Hell is Empty, All the Devils are Here	5/25/62
62. From an Enchantress Fleeing	6/1/62

#31. A Month of Sundays

Executive Producer: **Herbert B. Leonard**
Written by: **Stirling Silliphant**
Directed by: **Arthur Hiller**

Tod and Buz, employed in a Montana copper mine, rent rooms at Lydia Sullivan's home. Then Lydia's niece, Arline Simms arrives. Arline, a famous actress, has run out on a Broadway hit to return to her home town. She is completely silent about her reasons for doing so. Tod and Buz are attracted to Arline, and both compete for her attention. After many attempts Buz manages to date Arline, but Tod keeps trying. He follows Arline when she goes to church to see her old friend, Father Prior. Tod is trapped behind a pillar, and unable to leave without being observed.

Tod hears Arline tell Father Prior that she is suffering from a rare blood disease and has been told she will die in a few weeks. Although her acts have been evidence of a deep emotional problem, Arline has kept the secret to herself. Tod doesn't tell Buz.

Then Buz, who has fallen in love with Arline, shows Tod an engagement ring he has purchased. Before Buz arrives, Tod tells Arline and advises her to accept it. Later, while dancing, Buz gives the ring to Arline. Arline accepts it and falls to the floor. Buz phones for an ambulance. Tod arrives with Father Prior, and Arline dies.

Cast: Tod (*Martin Milner*), Buz (*George Maharis*), Arline Simms (*Anne Francis*), Father Prior (*Conrad Nagel*), Lydia Sullivan (*Betty Garde*).

#32. Blue Murder

Executive Producer: **Herbert B. Leonard**
Written by: **Stirling Silliphant**
Directed by: **Arthur Hiller**

Tod and Buz deliver "Blue Murder," a wild stallion, to its new owner, Jim Bludge, a wealthy rancher. Jim's wife, Blossom, pleads with Jim's brothers, Frank and Cam, to get him to return the horse, which has the reputation of being a killer. However, Jim insists on keeping the horse. Later, hearing loud noises, Tod, Buz and Frank rush to the paddock. Cam lies across the fence, but Jim is dead. A horseshoe has left its bloody marks on his crushed body, and "Blue Murder" has escaped. Plans are made to trap and kill "Blue Murder." Tod, who saved the horse's life on the Owens ranch, feels he must kill the murdering beast himself. Then Cam returns with Frank's body across the front of his saddle. Frank has been smashed to death by the shoes of a horse. Cam swears to get the horse who killed his brothers.

Tod and Buz, feeling that their work is done, start back to the Owens ranch. However, they are troubled about the murders. They drive to a burned-out lodge. Cam is there with "Blue Murder." Cam has always been envious of his brothers, and always wanted Blossom. He has used a sledge hammer with a horseshoe attached to its head to kill his brothers. He is now trying to affix that shoe to "Blue Murder's" hoof. The arrival of Tod and Buz causes "Blue Murder" to go wild. He stomps Cam to death. Tod and Buz take "Blue Murder" back to the Owens ranch, leaving Blossom in her lonely world.

Cast: Tod (*Martin Milner*), Buz (*George Maharis*), Blossom (*Suzanne Pleshette*), Cam (*Claude Akins*), Jim (*Gene Evans*), Frank (*Harry Townes*).

#33. Good Night, Sweet Blues

Executive Producer: **Herbert B. Leonard**
Written by: **Will Lorin**
Directed by: **Jack Smight**

Driving near Pittsburgh, Tod and Buz swerve from the road to avoid a car which seems to be out of control. Jennie Henderson is in the car. She has suffered a heart attack. The courage she displays while Tod and Buz are getting an ambulance impresses them deeply. Concerned, they trace Jennie to her home. Although Jennie's doctor has told her she may live for years, Jennie has forced him to admit that she might pass away in a short time. Jennie is a widow; she hasn't any children. She feels her only family are the "Memphis Naturals," the band she sang with thirty years before. Two have become famous; the others have dropped out of sight. She feels that she has a week to live, and wants to hear the band once more. Jennie asks Tod and Buz to find the musicians; she has more than enough money to pay for the search. Tod and Buz accept the difficult assignment.

Their search takes them from coast-to-coast, from the heights of success to the depths of defeat, from recording studios to prison. The banjo player is dead, but his son, Hank Plummer, gladly takes his place. Finally, all are rounded up, except King Loomis, the great trombonist. Buz finds him shining shoes in New York. With his pride gone, Loomis tells Buz that he can't play anymore. However, the boys bring the King and the other players to Jennie's home. Surrounded by the men she loved, playing the music she loves, Jennie sings her own lullaby as she leaves the world.

Cast: Tod (*Martin Milner*), Buz (*George Maharis*), Jennie (*Ethel Waters*), King Loomis (*Juano Hernandez*), The Memphis Naturals: Lover (*Jo Jones*), Horace (*Frederick O'Neal*), Hank (*Bill Gunn*), Snooze (*Coleman Hawkins*), A.C. (*Roy Eldridge*).

#34. Birdcage on My Foot

Executive Producer: **Herbert B. Leonard**
Teleplay by: **Stirling Silliphant**
Directed by: **Elliott Silverstein**

While Tod and Buz are visiting Charlotte Lee on Boston's Beacon Street, Arnie breaks into the glove box of their car. When Arnie flees, Tod chases him into the arms of Lieut. Calder. Calder spots Arnie as a drug addict. Calder tells Tod, Buz and Charlotte that the young man is a hopeless case. Tod agrees to withdraw charges if Arnie accompanies Charlotte and himself to her home while he works through a "withdrawal," as a first step to rehabilitation. Both Calder and Buz warn them against trying to help Arnie; then Buz gets into the car and drives off.

Arnie is locked in the living room in Charlotte's apartment. Pleading for a "fix," Arnie tries every trick to escape. He finally succeeds, but Tod recaptures him. Charlotte and Tod are ready to admit defeat. Then Buz returns and takes over. A hithertofore hidden part of Buz's life is disclosed, as he expertly approaches the case. Buz stays with Arnie all night, as the young man is wracked by the tortures of an addict breaking the habit.

Arnie is helped by Buz's revelation of the dramatic part drug addiction played in his own life. Left an orphan, Buz was befriended by a man who later became an addict after the death of his son. Buz feels he could have helped him fight his addiction, but his failure to do so was responsible for his friend's eventual suicide. Buz is determined to succeed with Arnie. When morning comes, both Buz and Arnie have won their battle. Tod and Buz drive Arnie to a U.S. Public Health Hospital where Arnie determines to continue the battle to rehabilitate himself.

Cast: Tod (*Martin Milner*), Buz (*George Maharis*), Arnie (*Robert Duvall*), Charlotte (*Diana Millay*), Lieut. Calder (*Mike Kellin*).

#35. First Class Mouliak

Executive Producer: **Herbert B. Leonard**
Written by: **John Vlahos**
Directed by : **William Conrad**

In Cleveland, Tod and Buz find employment with Jack Kolodziedjczak, top furnace man at a steel mill. Jack, a widower, has a daughter Eva, and a son, Janosh, who is preparing to study medicine. Jack's best friend is Mike Palinski, another top furnace man. Janosh has been secretly seeing Terry Palinski, Mike's daughter. During a quarrel, Terry runs away from Janosh, falls from a high bluff, and is killed. Janosh flees in panic and returns home. When Terry's body is found, Mike swears to kill his daughter's murderer. After the funeral, Eva, Terry's best friend, visits the Palinski home and goes through the girl's belongings with Mrs. Palinski.

Eva and Mrs. Palinski find the dead girl's diary and learn that Terry and Janosh had been dating, and were to meet on the night the girl was killed. Eva warns her brother, and he runs away. Tod and Buz stop Mike when he tries to attack Jack. Jack vows to kill his own son if he proves to be a murderer. A search is started for Janosh. Tod and Buz find Janosh and decide that Jack has a right to see his own son before they call the police. When Jack hears Janosh's story, he realizes that his own dictatorial attitude has, in a large measure, been responsible for the tragedy. He decides to stand by Janosh no matter what happens.

Cast: Tod (*Martin Milner*), Buz (*George Maharis*), Jack (*Nehemiah Persoff*), Mike (*Martin Balsam*), Janosh (*Robert Redford*), Eva (*Nancy Malone*), Teresa (*Ann Dee*).

#36. Once to Every Man

Executive Producer: **Herbert B. Leonard**
Written by: **Frank L. Moss**
Directed by: **Arthur Hiller**

At Gloucester, Mass., Tod and Buz find employment with the Adams Boat Company. Leigh Adams manages the company which has been a family enterprise for over one hundred years. His daughter Prudence roams from country to country looking for that indefinable something which might, or might not, make her life complete. At the launching of a new schooner, with his mother watching, Leigh is accidentally thrown in the water. Although Tod and Buz make every effort to safe his life, Leigh dies. Prudence comes home for her father's funeral, planning to return to Rome immediately. After the funeral she decides to dispose of the shipyard which has become an unprofitable enterprise. Her grandmother insists that she talk to the men in the shipyard and thank Tod and Buz for their efforts to save her father's life.

Prudence meets Tod. She feels that he is everything in life she wants. Although Buz warns him, Tod really falls for her. After a whirlwind courtship, Tod tells Buz that he and Prudence are to be married. Tod hopes to assume an active part in revitalizing the shipyard. Then Prudence, self-willed, starts to remake Tod's life. She tells Tod she is returning to Europe, with him of course, after their wedding. On hearing that Prudence has decided to close the shipyard, Tod breaks with her. Tod and Buz return to the open road.

Cast: Tod (*Martin Milner*), Buz (*George Maharis*), Prudence (*Janice Rule*), Leigh Adams (*Murray Matheson*), Grandmother (*Ann Shoemaker*).

#37. The Mud Nest

Executive Producer: **Herbert B. Leonard**
Written by: **Stirling Silliphant**
Directed by: **James Sheldon**

After leaving Interstate 95, Tod and Buz run out of gas at Hester, Maryland. Old natives see a striking resemblance in Buz to members of the Colby family. Buz has never known his parents. Puzzled by the reception, Buz drives out with Tod to see the Colbys. After Buz wins a fight with several Colby sons, grandpa Colby is emphatic that Buz is a member of their clan; and is the son of Dorothea Colby, who ran away to Baltimore with a man named Wallace shortly before Buz was born. Feeling that he at last might find his mother, Buz drives to Baltimore with Tod. Tod and Buz meet Lieut. Tegeler, of the Police Department's Missing Persons Bureau. Tegeler helps Buz and Tod trace every possible lead to find the long-lost Dorothea Colby.

Although evidence points to the fact that Dorothea must have hated her son, Buz pushes ahead with the search. Finally the trail leads them to Johns Hopkins Hospital, where they find that the long-lost Dorothea, who has changed her name to Joan Thompson, is employed as a nurse. Buz talks to Dorothea. For a moment he feels she may be his mother. However, she confesses to Buz that her child died when he was six weeks old. Afterwards she had become a nurse. Although Buz and Dorothea realize in that moment what might have been for each of them, Buz knows his search is over, and he leaves with Tod.

Cast: Tod (*Martin Milner*), Buz (*George Maharis*), Dorothea Colby (*Betty Field*), Colby (*Lon Chaney, Jr.*), Lt. Tegeler (*Edward Asner*).

#38. A Bridge Across Five Days

Executive Producer: **Herbert B. Leonard**
Written by: **Howard Rodman**
Directed by: **Richard Donner**

Employed in a Baltimore shipyard with Tod, Buz becomes involved in an argument with Mrs. Lillian Aldrich, a personnel employee who has told him his Social Security number is wrong. When Lillian breaks into tears and runs from the office, Buz is completely puzzled. Late that night, Buz receives a disjointed phone call from Lillian which baffles him even more. Next morning, Buz goes to the personnel office to apologize. Learning that Lillian hasn't come to work, Buz gets the address of the boarding house where she lives, and drives there with Tod. Mr. Mexia, the owner of the boarding house, tells them that everyone residing there has been confined to a mental hospital at one time or another.

Lillian has recently been released after being in a local mental hospital for eighteen years. She was married and the mother of an infant girl at the time she was committed. Since then her husband had divorced her and raised the child, believing her mother to be dead. Her daughter is now married. The day of the altercation with Buz was the first day Lillian worked since her release from the institution. Buz and Tod become friends with Lillian. As a result, Lillian returns to work.

Then Lillian tries to see her daughter, Mrs. Josephine Ryan. Her daughter refuses to accept Lillian. Lillian asks Tod and Buz to take her back to the mental institution. After Lillian enters the hospital, Buz asks Tod to wait a half hour or so. Lillian realizes that the institution is no longer her home, and returns to the world she feels she has the courage to accept.

Cast: Tod (*Martin Milner*), Buz (*George Maharis*), Lillian (*Nina Foch*), Mexia (*James Dunn*), Beatrice Ware (*Jean Muir*), Jo (*Davey Davison*), Paul Guin (*James Patterson*).

#39. Mon Petit Chou

Executive Producer: **Herbert B. Leonard**
Written by: **Stirling Silliphant**
Directed by: **Sam Peckinpah**

Tod and Buz find employment on a dredge, working the Ohio River, near Pittsburgh. There, Tod meets and falls for Perette Dijon, singing protégé of Ryan, a talented impresario. Ryan's soul is warped by his experience with his former wife. He had developed her into a singing star; her unfaithfulness had resulted in her own ruin and crushed his dreams. Now he has discovered Perette, and tutored her to the edge of singing greatness. Perette loves him, but Ryan twisted by his past experience and determined to never fall in love again, treats her in a brutal impersonal manner. Feeling that her situation is hopeless, Perette turns to Tod. Higgy Carson, Ryan's assistant, warns Tod to keep away from the girl. Ryan finds Tod and Perette together. Ryan savagely knocks Tod out and locks Perette in her room. He warns Perette that if he ever finds her with another man he will kill her.

Tod tells Buz that he is determined to even the score with Ryan. Tod and Buz drive to Le Mont, where Perette is singing. Challenged by Tod, Ryan follows him to the parking lot. Tod beats Ryan in a savage fight. Perette tries to comfort Ryan to break through the barrier he has built between them. As he shouts his hate for the woman who betrayed him, Ryan becomes aware of the sincerity of Perette's love and devotion. Later, Tod and Buz listen as Perette, inspired by the triumph of her love, gives her greatest performance.

Cast: Tod (*Martin Milner*), Buz (*George Maharis*), Glenn Ryan (*Lee Marvin*), Perette Dijon (*Macha Meril*), Higgy (*Bert Remsen*).

#40. Some of the People, Some of the Time

Executive Producer: **Herbert B. Leonard**
Written by: **Stirling Silliphant**
Directed by: **Robert Altman**

Tod and Buz take jobs with Max Coyne. Max travels from town to town with his wife Caroline, and a three-piece band, setting up beauty contests. The winner is guaranteed a role in a Hollywood movie. Max actually gets some of the contestants roles through a contact in a major studio. Since it is believed that Tod and Buz can influence the outcome, they become targets for every would-be contestant when the troupe arrives in Carlisle, Pa. Tod meets Jahala West, a plain-looking waitress. Feeling sorry for her, he determines to help her win. Then Caroline learns Max's Hollywood contact has been fired by the studio. She pleads with Max to give up their precarious life and settle down to a more normal existence. But Max tells Caroline he is determined to find somebody else in Hollywood to guarantee the winner of the contest an acting part.

With Max, Tod and Buz working at top speed, the contest is put on at the local high school auditorium. Then Mrs. Pearson arrives with her daughter, Cynthia, who had won a previous contest conducted by Max. In Hollywood with Cynthia, Mrs. Pearson had discovered that Max's friend had been fired. Just as Jahala is crowned Miss Carlisle, Mrs. Pearson appears and breaks up the contest. Max and his associates, including Tod and Buz, are thrown into the local jail. Then Caroline arrives. She has taken Max's career into her own hands and gotten him a job in Hollywood as a third assistant director. Max and his group are released from jail. Tod and Buz bid farewell to Max who vows to have the studio in the palm of his hand within six months.

Cast: Tod (*Martin Milner*), Buz (*George Maharis*), Max Coyne (*Keenan Wynn*), Jahala West (*Lois Nettleton*), Caroline Coyne (*Shirl Conway*), Mrs. Pearson (*Jane Hoffman*).

#41. The Thin White Line

Executive Producer: **Herbert B. Leonard**
Written by: **Leonard Freeman**
Directed by: **David Lowell Rich**

Tod and Buz attend a party in Philadelphia. Harold, their student host, hates one of his guests and spikes his beer with a hallucinogen that induces a severe psychotic state. Tod inadvertently drinks the beer. Tod suddenly becomes a raging maniac. He sends Buz crashing against a wall when his friend tries to stop him, then crashes through a window and races out into the night. Dr. Anderson, Harold's professor, is called. He phones the police and tells them that Tod, in an induced psychotic state, is potentially dangerous to others and to himself. Tod roams the city, suffering every type of weird hallucination. Dr. Anderson tells Buz that the effect may last six to eight hours and that the final phase is one of depression in which the victim might try to kill himself.

Police cars patrol the streets in a frantic search for Tod. Tod enters Nicky's basement bar. Realizing they are dealing with a mad man, the bartender and patrons give in to Tod's every whim, fearful of what he might do. Finally, Red, one of the girls, takes Tod to her apartment. Suddenly Tod's mood changes. He visualizes Red as a fearsome Medusa and rushes to the street. A police car spots Tod. With Buz, Doctor Anderson, and the police closing in, Tod climbs the Ben Franklin Bridge. High above the Delaware River, the urge for self-destruction seizes Tod. Risking death, Buz manages to get to Tod. He leads him from the edge of death to safety. Hours later, Tod awakens in a hospital room, once more himself.

Cast: Tod (*Martin Milner*), Buz (*George Maharis*), Dr. Anderson (*Murray Hamilton*), Officer Romero (*Fred J. Scollay*), Joe (*Al Lewis*), Red (*Sylvia Miles*), Nancy (*Anita Gillette*).

#42. And The Cat Jumped Over the Moon

Executive Producer: **Herbert B. Leonard**
Written by: **Sterling Silliphant**
Directed by: **Elliot Silverstein**

In Philadelphia, Tod and Buz visit Chuck Brennan, a social worker and long-time friend of Buz. He is now working with the "Missiles," a juvenile gang who make their headquarters in a new housing development. Packy, a vicious eighteen year old, inherited the leadership of the gang from Johnny Berenson after Johnny was persuaded by Chuck to become a useful member of society. As leader, Packy, in accordance with the gang's code, expects to inherit John's girlfriend Marva. Packy learns that Johnny and Marva plan to marry. He decides to lead the gang in punishing Johnny for this infraction of rules.

Tod and Buz are unaware of this when Marva gets Chuck to leave his apartment to stop the gang. Chuck accepts Packy's challenge to a duel of "follow the leader"—running around and jumping from parapet to parapet of the apartment building. Chuck falls to his death. At police headquarters, Packy's story that Chuck's death was accidental is corroborated by a witness. Packy and the gang are released.

Questioned by Tod and Buz, Marva reveals the reasons behind Chuck's death. Buz leaves Tod and Marva in Brennan's apartment while he looks for Johnny. He returns with Johnny to find that Tod has been beaten by the gang, and that Packy has pursued Marva to the roof. Although Buz insists it is his right to avenge Chuck's death, Johnny overrules him. In a contest similar to the one in which Chuck met his death, Packy turns "chicken" and is mauled by the gang members. Tod and Buz leave Marva and Johnny who have at last freed themselves from the gang.

Cast: Tod (*Martin Milner*), Buz (*George Maharis*), Chuck Brennan (*Milt Kamen*), Marva (*Susan Silo*), Johnny (*James Caan*), Packy (*Martin Sheen*).

#43. Burning for Burning

Executive Producer: **Herbert B. Leonard**
Written by: **Stirling Silliphant**
Directed by: **Charles Haas**

Widowed at an early age, Mrs. Agnes Brack's struggle to raise her family and keep her husband's farm has turned her into a stern, implacable matriarch who rules her family with an iron hand. She has broken the spirit of her son Frank and his wife Beth. Only her daughter Laura has managed to retain some semblance of her own integrity. Some months before Tod and Buz are hired by Mrs. Brack, she receives word that her younger son Mark, who left home to escape his mother, has drowned in Europe. Now Julia, his young widow, arrives unexpectedly at the Penna. farm with her three-month-old baby. Mrs. Brack tells Julia that Mark was a weakling, unable to care for himself. She adds that there is no place at the farm for Julia and orders her to return to Europe with her baby. Frank, determined to hold onto his anticipated inheritance of the farm, also does everything possible to drive Julia away.

Tod and Buz help Julia to find a place to live in the town, made unfriendly by Frank's unfounded attacks on Julia's character. Laura defies her mother, visits Julia and brings the baby back to the farm. Feeling she is being tricked, Mrs. Brack returns the baby to Julia. Under Mrs. Brack's attack, Julia admits she came to the farm to turn the baby over to Mrs. Brack for a price. But she adds that she will not now, under any circumstance, give Mrs. Brack another man-child to destroy. She destroys Mrs. Brack's defense completely when she tells her that Mark drowned trying to prove his manhood, not to himself or his wife, but to his mother. Mrs. Brack breaks and she asks Julia to remain with her baby. Tod and Buz leave the two women together.

Cast: Tod (*Martin Milner*), Buz (*George Maharis*), Julie (*Inger Stevens*), Agnes (*Beulah Bondi*), Frank (*Pat Hingle*), Laura (*Ann Dee*).

#44. To Walk with the Serpent

Executive Producer: **Herbert B. Leonard**
Written by: **Will Lorin**
Directed by: **James Sheldon**

While visiting historical sites near Boston, Tod and Buz meet John Westerbrook. Westerbrook is accompanied by a motorcycle escort and entourage composed of Emery Williams, Amelia Van Ness, and Jack Davis. The group gives the impression of being a private army. Westerbrook insists on guiding Tod and Buz. Later, driving away, Tod and Buz become aware that they are being followed. Their pursuer proves to be a government agent. He takes them to Ben Newcombe, a special agent. Newcombe shows them motion pictures of Westerbrook's activities, and convinces them that Westerbrook is trying to overthrow the government. They learn that the Westerbrook group has acquired enough plastic explosives to blow up two or three city blocks. Newcombe adds that the government agent who infiltrated the organization to learn its plans has been killed.

Tod and Buz are introduced to Westerbrook's father, Henry Westerbrook, who tells them that his son is driven by a desire to destroy himself and everything around him. Tod and Buz agree to join Westerbrook's organization to discover its plans. They learn that Westerbrook has scheduled a mass meeting near a historical monument, and that the explosives are to be used to blow it up. This is to be Westerbrook's first step in his scheme to overthrow the government. As people gather, and the meeting starts, government operatives make a frantic search to find the explosives. Finally, Davis, who was to have fired the shot setting off the explosion, is discovered and killed. Westerbrook is captured and led away in a straightjacket.

Cast: Tod (*Martin Milner*), Buz (*George Maharis*), John Westerbrook (*Dan O'Herlihy*), Ben Newcombe (*Simon Oakland*), Henry Westerbrook (*Judson Laire*), Emery Williams (*Logan Ramsey*), Davis (*Frank Sutton*), Amelia Van Ness (*DeAnn Mears*), Perry Hall (*Joseph Campanella*).

#45. A Long Piece of Mischief

Executive Producer: **Herbert B. Leonard**
Written by: **Stirling Silliphant**
Directed by: **David Lowell Rich**

Joe Wiley's rodeo comes to Mesquite, Texas where Tod and Buz are employed by the Crown Brick Co. Ollie, the rodeo clown, was a top rider but lost his right arm in an arena accident some years before. His good nature makes him the butt of the rodeo horseplay, most of it good natured, but in the case of rodeo riders Del McNabb and Jud Higgins, extremely vicious. Ollie loves "Babe" Hunter, the rodeo queen. Buz and Tod save Ollie from one of Del's most brutal stunts, thereby earning Del's enmity. Although Jud tells Del they've badgered Ollie enough, Del persuades him to have one more go at the clown and take Buz in for good measure. Del tells Ollie that Babe is in love with him, that she's waiting for him to propose. Ollie agrees to ask Babe to marry him at the barbecue Del is giving that evening. Jud gets Babe drunk at a local bar and gives the manager orders to serve her drinks until she passes out.

Ollie invites Tod and Buz to the barbecue. At the barbecue, a girl lures Buz away from Tod. A cowboy lassoes him and he is taken to Babe's trailer. After Buz is bound and gagged, Del puts Babe's negligee on him. Ollie makes a long plea of his affections to Babe, unaware that he is talking to Buz. The concealed merrymakers break out in roars of laughter. Jud tells Ollie that Babe thought up the scheme. Ollie is humiliated and decides to leave the rodeo. Buz tells him that's just what Del wants. Suddenly, Ollie realizes he is not a failure, hiding behind the mask of a clown. The next day he makes his greatest appearance in the arena. Later, Tod and Buz watch the rodeo pull out with Ollie and Babe, who at last found love together.

Cast: Tod (*Martin Milner*), Buz (*George Maharis*), Ollie (*Albert Salmi*), Babe (*Audrey Totter*), Del (*Ben Johnson*), Jud (*Slim Pickens*), Wylie (*Denver Pyle*).

#46. 1800 Days to Justice

Executive Producer: **Herbert B. Leonard**
Written by: **Jo Pagano**
Directed by: **David Lowell Rich**

After spending five years in jail, David Job, accompanied by his mob, rides into Harcourt Juncture, a small oil town in Texas. He takes command of the telephone office connecting the town with the outside world, and also seizes the wives of prominent citizens as hostages. Shortly after, Tod and Buz drive into town. Word of Job's return spreads, reaching his brother Emlyn and his former girlfriend Ann. Job is waiting for the train from San Antonio. He knows Bob Harcourt who practically owns the town is on the train. Job takes Harcourt to the courthouse. There, the citizens of Harcourt Juncture, surrounded by Job's men, are forced to put Harcourt on trial for railroading Job to jail. Job appoints Tod to be Harcourt's lawyer.

Job is shocked however, when Ann, after admitting she left him for Harcourt, swears that she couldn't testify in Job's behalf because his own attorney who had sold him out, had refused to allow her to do so. Although fearful of the revenge the Harcourts might take against them, the people vote Harcourt guilty. Then Job tells them that he is going to shoot Harcourt. Buz gets Job to agree to fight him for Harcourt's life. Although Job beats Buz to a pulp, his brother Emlyn makes him realize that it would be foolish to kill Harcourt and sacrifice his future and the affection of his neighbors. Job beats down a move made by members of his mob to take over. Tod and Buz leave Job and Ann to make a new life for themselves.

Cast: Tod (*Martin Milner*), Buz (*George Maharis*), David (*John Ericson*), Emlyn (*Noah Beery*), Ann (*Marion Ross*), Harcourt (*DeForest Kelley*).

#47. City of Wheels

Executive Producer: **Herbert B. Leonard**
Written by: **Frank Chase**
Directed by: **David Lowell Rich**

Tod and Buz, employed at the Long Beach Veterans Hospital, meet Frank Madera, a paraplegic. After Frank, a fighter pilot, was seriously injured in a plane crash, his wife left him. Although other paraplegics at the hospital are adjusting to their condition, Frank is extremely bitter. Lori Barton, employed at the hospital, has fallen in love with Frank, but he repels her every effort to get close to him. When Tod dates Midge Doran, Lori and Buz join them at a local nightclub. Frank and Smudge, also a paraplegic, enter the nightclub in their wheelchairs. There Buz's ability to chase a young drunk who has made a play for Lori, intensifies Frank's bitterness. Lori tells Buz she loves Frank, but is leaving the hospital because of his attitude. Buz tries to get through to Frank, but all his efforts are defeated. However, he tells him that Lori is leaving the hospital.

Frank visits Lori's office to see her before she leaves. She tries to make him realize the sincerity of her love, but Frank, afraid it would never work, leaves. He wheels himself to the hospital swimming pool. After securing the belt of his wheelchair tightly about him, he wheels off into the deep water. Buz, after a tremendous struggle, rescues Frank. Although Buz reports that the occurrence was an accident, Frank tells the doctor the truth. He thanks Buz for saving his life, which has finally become very important to him. Frank, who has gained a purpose in life, wheels himself toward Lori, ready to fight all odds to win happiness for both of them.

Cast: Tod (*Martin Milner*), Buz (*George Maharis*), Frank Madera (*Steven Hill*), Lori (*Bethel Leslie*), Smudge (*James Callahan*), Midge (*Jacqueline Scott*), Dan (*John Lasell*).

#48. How Much a Pound is Albatross?

Executive Producer: **Herbert B. Leonard**
Written by: **Stirling Silliphant**
Directed by: **David Lowell Rich**

In Tucson, Vicki Russell, driving her motorcycle recklessly at top speed, forces Tod and Buz from the road. They crash into a store window. Motorcycle police close in on Vicki and find she has neither license plates nor an operator's license. She is taken to the sheriff's office. Little by little, the reason for Vicki's out-of-the-world attitude toward life is revealed. Vicki, an heiress to a great fortune, has lost her whole family in an air crash and she has been speeding from place to place, trying to find some reason for living. Vicki is jailed to await trial. Touched by the girl's plight, Buz persuades Tod to use their car as collateral to raise bail for her release.

Upon release, Vicki finds—at least for the moment—something that she has been looking for in Tod. He gets her motorcycle from the garage the night before she is to appear in court, and they ride into the desert. The motorcycle breaks down, and they are forced to battle for their lives against man's most inexorable enemy—nature itself. Buz joins a huge search party to find Tod and Vicki.

The judge, after weighing all the incidents responsible for Vicki's mental state, suspends sentence on the condition that she leaves town within the next hour. At the end of the highway leading to nowhere, at least for Vicki, Tod and Buz watch the girl drive off on her reckless search for that indefinable meaning of life, sometimes elusive for many of us.

Cast: Tod (*Martin Milner*), Buz (*George Maharis*), Vicki (*Julia Newmar*), Landers (*Frank McHugh*).

#49. Aren't You Surprised to See Me?

Executive Producer: Herbert B. Leonard
Written by: Stirling Silliphant
Directed by: James Sheldon

Tod and Buz get jobs in Dallas, Texas. Shortly after, Caine, posing as John Farrington, arrives. He immediately telegraphs the Mayor of Dallas that the city is on trial. The police are alerted and spring into action to catch him. Caine is a madman who believes he is the avenging angel of the Almighty. He goes from town to town, searching until he finds a man whom he believes is his brother. He keeps that person captive for twenty-four hours. If at that time he believes the town has been free from sin for the period, he releases his captive. If the papers report one sinful act, he kills his prisoner and assumes the man's identity. He has killed six men.

Caine sees Buz and believes he is the man to be held hostage until Dallas proves itself free of sin. Tod alerts the police who find clues that Buz is with Caine. Newspapers, television and radio cooperate in refraining from publishing or broadcasting any type of news that could trigger Caine into action. Meanwhile, Tod and the police search frantically to get to Buz before Caine kills him. Finally, Caine finds a piece of news which leads him to believe the town has broken its act of faith. He prepares to kill Buz. Buz breaks away. A chase ensues, and the police close in. Trapped, Caine kills himself. Buz and Tod stand together once more.

Cast: Tod (*Martin Milner*), Buz (*George Maharis*), Caine (*David Wayne*), Captain Strode (*James Brown*).

#50. You Never Had It So Good

Executive Producer: **Herbert B. Leonard**
Written by: **Stirling Silliphant and Frank L. Moss**
Directed by: **James Sheldon**

David Leland (Lee) Fisk, thirty-two, heads one of the country's largest development enterprises. Terry Prentiss, beautiful and ambitious, is his assistant. Terry, running tests to find a new Eastern Vice-President, decides to recruit the man from within the company itself. Rifling through the employee files, Terry comes across Tod Stiles' name. Tod and Buz are working as laborers. Tod refuses the new assignment, but Buz is eager to meet Terry. Tod sends Buz in his place.

Interested more in Terry than the job, Buz goes along with her plans. Buz tells Lee he knows nothing about the company's nefarious operations. Lee tells him he'll soon learn. Terry supervises a cram course in the company's operations for Buz. She advises him to talk up at the staff meetings. Finally, Buz presents an extremely ambitious plan. It is Terry's plan, but she has insisted that Buz present it. Lee is impressed. He takes Buz along to set the deal in operation.

Buz realizes he is being trapped in a way of life that is just not for him. He gives Lee his resignation. Terry startles Lee by revealing that she knew Buz wasn't right for the job, but had set him up as a strawman so she could prove her own fitness. Lee, realizing he loves Terry, asks her to marry him. Although Terry insists on having the position, Lee insists he will eventually marry her. Buz rejoins Tod.

Cast: Tod (*Martin Milner*), Buz (*George Maharis*), Lee (*Peter Graves*), Terry (*Patricia Barry*).

#51. Shoulder the Sky, My Lad

Executive Producer: **Herbert B. Leonard**
Written by: **Mort Thaw**
Directed by: **David Lowell Rich**

In Phoenix, Tod and Buz find employment in a factory. Their foreman, Carl Selman, is a widower. Carl lives with his mother, Annie Selman, and his thirteen-year-old son Davey. The Selmans are Jewish. Davey is preparing for his bar mitzvah. Carl is stabbed to death by two dope addicts. Davey is inconsolable. Rabbi Harris tries, but is unable to alleviate his grief. Tod and Buz try to do everything possible to help Mrs. Selman and Davey.

After his father's funeral, Davey runs away. Tod and Buz search fruitlessly for him. Davey goes to the home of his schoolmate Rose Corbello. He tells her that he is going to board a freight train and go to San Francisco where he hopes to become a sailor. Tod and Buz find Davey standing before his father's grave. Davey tries to run away, but Buz captures him. As Buz relates his own feelings on being orphaned, Davey regains his own faith and belief in God. Carl's killers are captured. Later Buz and Tod are present at Davey's bar mitzvah.

Cast: Tod (*Martin Milner*), Buz (*George Maharis*), Annie Selman (*Lili Darvas*), Rose Corbello (*Susan Gordon*), Davey Selman (*Mike McGreevey*), Carl Selman (*Edward Asner*).

#52. Blues for a Left Foot

Executive Producer: **H. B. Leonard**
Written by: **Leonard Freeman**
Directed by: **Arthur Hiller**

During his college years, Tod falls in love with Rosemarie Brown. When the show in which she is the star dancer plays in New Haven, Rosemarie tells him she is engaged to marry Dave Mann, also appearing in the show. Years later Tod and Buz find employment in a Hollywood television studio. Meanwhile, Mann, after marrying Rosemarie, reaches the top in the theatrical field. Sickened by that most poisonous of all diseases, success, Dave takes to drink and dies an alcoholic's death. Tod and Buz attend his funeral.

Tod and Buz find that Rosemarie has been deserted by all the sycophants who paid court to Dave while he was riding high. Tod and Buz persuade Sam Benjamin, a television producer, to give Rosemarie a tryout for one of his reviews. All of Rosemarie's self-confidence is gone. Tod and Buz try to help her regain courage. Peter Marlin, the star comic of the show, whose own laughs come from the hurts suffered by others, promises to help her get a part. After her back is turned, he gives orders to keep her from the set.

Tod and Buz go all out for Rosemarie, even though, her confidence is shaken further when she sees dancers Rhoda, Joy, and Maxine perform. Rosemarie gains strength, especially when Sam Benjamin, who remembers her, stops Marlin from depriving her from her chance for a comeback. Tod and Buz return to their duties as stagehands on the set after seeing Rosemarie make a triumphal success.

Cast: Tod (*Martin Milner*), Buz (*George Maharis*), Rosemarie (*Elizabeth Seal*), Sam Benjamin (*Akim Tamiroff*), Pete Marlin (*Zack Matalon*).

#53. Go Read the River

Executive Producer: **H. B. Leonard**
Written by: **Stirling Silliphant**
Directed by: **Arthur Hiller**

Tod and Buz are employed by McCullough Aircraft Corporation. When the front office learns of Tod's experience racing boats, he is assigned to assist Sandy Mason in testing a revolutionary hydro-engine for speedboats. Ten years before, Sandy's wife, confused by his dedication to his work, left him and took their daughter Dana with her. Sandy retreated into his own world, determined to prove that he needed neither wife nor friends.

Since Sandy's engine will revolutionize racing, efforts are made by other companies to learn the secret of this design. Sandy and Tod fly to Lake Havasu for preliminary tests before the final McCullough Marathon. Sandy's daughter, Dana, comes to the lake. She keeps secret the fact that her mother and stepfather have been killed. She is alone and terrified by the world. She tries to communicate with her father, but his bitterness at what he feels was his wife's betrayal is a bar between them.

Tod, touched by the girl's tragic plight, tries but fails to bring father and daughter together. Shortly before the big race, Tod learns that Dana, with all hope gone, is about to leave. As Sandy is about to step into his racing craft, Tod makes him listen to his daughter's story. Dana has already left. Sandy makes his big decision. He turns his boat over to Tod and Bob Keel to race, which they do triumphantly, while he races after his daughter.

Cast: Tod (*Martin Milner*), Buz (*George Maharis*), Sandy (*John Larch*), Dana (*Lois Smith*), Bob Keel (*Russell Johnson*).

#54. Even Stones Have Eyes

Executive Producer: **H. B. Leonard**
Written by: **Barry Trivers**
Directed by: **Robert Gist**

Tod and Buz are employed by a construction company building a skyscraper in Austin, Texas. A girder clips Buz on the back of his head while he is working high above street level. Tod saves him from certain death. On regaining consciousness, Buz finds that he cannot see. Eye specialists feel there is a chance he will be blind for life. Buz becomes extremely bitter and thinks about committing suicide. He runs away from Tod. When he falls to the street, Sam, a blind news dealer, comes to his aid. Sam tells him he learned how to face life in Kerrville. Tod drives Buz to the institution Sam talked about.

Buz meets Frank Robinson, the executive director in charge of the rehabilitation program. He learns that Robinson is blind. Robinson assigns Celia Montera as counselor to Buz. Celia is also blind. Slowly, Buz's innate courage comes to the fore and he starts fighting back against cruel fate. Celia falls in love with Buz. She tells Robinson. He tells her to continue as Buz's instructor.

Buz learns that Celia is in love with him and decides to leave the institution. Celia feels she has destroyed him. She runs away and falls into a lake. She can't swim. Buz follows and during his efforts in saving Celia, regains his sight.

Later, Buz says good-bye to Celia. He learns that she has enrolled at the University of Texas and promises to return.

Cast: Tod (*Martin Milner*), Buz (*George Maharis*), Celia (*Barbara Barrie*), Frank Robinson (*Paul Tripp*), Dr. Snyder (*Booth Colman*), Chet Hollis (*Dallas Mitchell*).

#55. Love is a Skinny Kid

Executive Producer: **H. B. Leonard**
Written by: **Stirling Silliphant**
Directed by: **James Sheldon**

Tod and Buz are forced to spend a few hours in Kilkenny, a small Texas town. A young girl wearing a Japanese mask gets off a bus. Her arrival starts a chaotic series of events in the town as she goes from place to place wearing the mask. She places an ad in Jason Palmer's weekly newspaper. The ad invites the whole town to attend a commemorative ceremony for Miriam Moore at Lydia Manning's home. When she tells Palmer that she's Miriam Moore's friend, Palmer tells her Miriam has been dead and buried for a long time.

Lydia Manning demands that Sheriff Bruner force the girl to leave town. Tod wants to leave, but Buz, feeling the girl in the mask is being driven by deep hatred, insists on staying to help her. Befriended, the girl reveals that she is Miriam Moore and that Lydia Manning is her mother. Miriam was an unwanted child; Lydia committed her to an asylum.

When she planned to re-marry, Lydia felt she must keep secret the fact that she had a daughter in an asylum. She publicly announced that Miriam had died in the asylum. After confronting Lydia, Miriam feels she has accomplished her mission. Tod and Buz drive her away from the town which believed her to be dead.

Cast: Tod (*Martin Milner*), Buz (*George Maharis*), Miriam (*Tuesday Weld*), Lydia (*Cloris Leachman*), Tommy (*Burt Reynolds*), Sheriff Bruner (*Malcolm Atterbury*), Jason Palmer (*Harry Townes*).

#56. Kiss the Maiden All Forlorn

Executive Producer: **H. B. Leonard**
Written by: **Stirling Silliphant**
Directed by: **David Lowell Rich**

Police start searching all entrances to Dallas when news is received that Charles Clayton has returned to the country. Eight years have passed since Clayton fled to escape imprisonment for embezzling millions. Even Howard Davis, a newspaper reporter who covered the case, can't fathom Clayton's reason for coming back and facing imprisonment. Tod and Buz stop on a highway outside of Dallas to help a girl whose car has stalled. The girl is Clayton's daughter, Bonnie. Antonio and Elena drive up. They are employed by Clayton. Antonio pulls out a gun and forces Tod, Buz and Bonnie to accompany them to the Holiday Inn.

Meanwhile, Clayton has eluded all law enforcement officers by landing in a seaplane on a nearby lake. Clayton has learned that his daughter plans to become a nun. Feeling that she is the sole heir to the fortune he has created, he determines to do everything to stop her. He goes to the Holiday Inn. He is unable to force Bonnie to change her plans. He even goes to see Mother Teresa at the Holy Trinity Convent to try to get her to stop Bonnie from becoming a nun. Finally, he is forced to accept defeat, and does so graciously. Tod and Buz, even Davis, are in a position to stop Clayton from leaving the country, but are reluctant to do so. They watch the seaplane carrying Clayton rise above the lake and disappear from view.

Cast: Tod (*Martin Milner*), Buz (*George Maharis*), Charles Clayton (*Douglas Fairbanks, Jr.*), Howard (*Arthur Hill*), Bonnie (*Zina Bethune*), Elena (*Elena Verdugo*), Antonio (*Michael Tolan*).

#57. Two on the House

Executive Producer: **H. B. Leonard**
Written by: **Gil Ralston**
Directed by: **David Lowell Rich**

Tod and Buz get jobs on the Carol Dianne II, a Lake Erie excursion boat, skippered by Asa Turnbull. Twelve-year-old Richie McIntyre is among a group of pupils escorted aboard the boat for a cruise. Richie is the only child of construction tycoon Willard McIntyre, a widower. Involved in running his huge construction enterprise, McIntyre has completely forgotten his son and now is scheduled to leave for North Africa to supervise another job. Richie falls overboard. Tod and Buz rescue him. They are more than surprised when Richie claims he was pushed.

The police are called, and Richie's father is notified. Tod and Buz and the passengers are questioned as to their part in the attempted murder. Meanwhile McIntyre receives a threatening note warning him that what happened to his son is but a prelude. Garrison, a police officer, suggests McIntyre take Richie to Africa with him, but he refuses. Then Richie finds what appears to be proof that his father has gone to Africa. Although Richie is constantly guarded at the McIntyre's home, he runs away. A city-wide search starts for Richie.

Richie makes his way to the Carol Dianne II, and asks for a job on the boat. He tells Tod and Buz that he jumped overboard, and wrote the first and subsequent threatening letters to his father, hoping to keep him at home. Tod and Buz finally bring father and son together. McIntyre at last realizes that no job is as important as the love of his son.

Cast: Tod (*Martin Milner*), Buz (*George Maharis*), Willard McIntyre (*Ralph Meeker*), Asa Turnbull (*Henry Jones*), Richie (*Brad Herrman*), Garrison (*Herbert Voland*).

#58. There I Am, There I Always Am

Executive Producer: **H. B. Leonard**
Written by: **Stirling Silliphant**
Directed by: **John Newland**

During a party aboard Emil Barraux's yacht, Lola asks for a new island, someplace her young but sophisticated eyes have never seen. Barraux points to Catalina Island. Champagne bottle in hand, Lola jumps overboard and starts for shore. Meantime, Tod and Buz have been skin-diving from the island. After Tod drives to town, Buz sees Lola come out of the water. Lola tells Buz she came ashore because she thought the island was uninhabited. Buz draws a line of demarcation in the sand and informs her that the other side is all hers.

Lola wanders away. Her ankle gets stuck between rocks as the tide starts coming in. Buz becomes aware of her predicament. However, every effort he makes to free the girl fails. He tries to contact someone, anyone, but lines of communication are cut. As the tide comes in Lola realizes she may drown. As the waters rise higher, Buz works frantically to free her to no avail. At one point, it seems Buz will have to cut her free to save her life, but loses his knife in the surf. Then Barraux's yacht approaches. Buz's shouts reach the yacht. Barraux sees him waving.

Using grappling hooks, Barraux and his skipper help Buz release Lola. For a moment, Lola feels she may stay with Buz and his kind of life. Then she decides to leave in Barraux's dinghy for the yacht.

Cast: Tod (*Martin Milner*), Buz (*George Maharis*), Lola (*Joanna Moore*), Emil Barraux (*Emile Genest*).

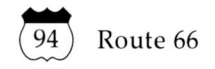

#59. Between Hello and Goodbye

Executive Producer: **H. B. Leonard**
Written by: **Stirling Silliphant**
Directed by: **David Lowell Rich**

In Southern California, Tod meets beautiful, blonde Christine Sinclair in a small night spot. She maneuvers Tod into a fight with another patron, then leaves. Later, Claire, a brunette, tells Tod that Christine is her sister. Claire is being treated by Dr. Reisman, a psychiatrist. A whole area of Claire's background escapes Dr. Reisman. He asks Claire to bring Christine to his office, hoping to learn more about their family. Tod meets Chris again, and they become deeply involved with each other. Claire pleads with Tod to break with Chris. She tells him that the romance with her sister can only lead to Tod's destruction.

Tod finally realizes that Chris is a very sick girl. He locks her in a room while he tries to make contact with Dr. Reisman. Tod returns with the psychiatrist. Chris eludes them, gets into a car, and drives wildly to Pacific Ocean Park, an amusement center. She enters the gondola of a sky ride. Far above, she threatens to jump out. Reisman, having pieced everything together, realizes that Chris and Claire are the same girl, and that Claire is trying to kill the part of her she hates. Realizing the truth of Reisman's shouted discovery, Claire returns to the ground. Tod leaves her with the man he hopes will eventually cure her.

Cast: Tod (*Martin Milner*), Claire/Chris (*Susan Oliver*), Dr. Arthur Reisman (*Herschel Bernardi*), Man in Nightclub (*Steve Peck*), Mr. Martin (*Ralph Barnard*), Mrs. Martin (*Ruth Enders*), Mrs. Thomas (*Joan Tompkins*).

#60. A Feat of Strength

Executive Producer: **H. B. Leonard**
Written by: **Howard Rodman and Joseph Petracca**
Directed by: **David Lowell Rich**

Tod gets a job as assistant to Steiner, a wrestling promoter, confined to a wheelchair. Steiner and Tod drive to the bus depot to meet Sandor, a Hungarian wrestler who was a great champion in his native country. Sandor, a patriot, has been in jail in Hungary for five years for fighting the government. He had expected his wife Eva to meet him. He believes she owns an inn. Steiner and Tod drive him to the inn. Sandor hasn't seen his wife in 8 years. He believes it was her money that was responsible for his release from jail.

Eva tells Sandor she gave all their funds to a general who promised to win Sandor's release, but the general disappeared with the money. She tells Sandor that she lied, that she only works at the inn. Steiner fell in love with Eva. Steiner promised to win Sandor's release on the condition that he wrestle for him. Sandor realizes that he is committed to fight as a Hungarian wrestler, appearing in fake matches.

Sandor's pride as a great champion is crushed. However, he knows that he must go on to win a final freedom for him and his wife. As Sandor leaves the ring after losing his first match, Tod realizes that Sandor has found the personal strength and courage that will result in victory for Eva and him.

Cast: Tod (*Martin Milner*), Sandor (*Jack Warden*), Eva (*Signe Hasso*), Steiner (*Joe de Santis*).

#61. Hell is Empty; All the Devils are Here

Executive Producer: **H. B. Leonard**
Written by: **Stirling Silliphant**
Directed by: **Paul Stanley**

Tod gets a job taking care of camels at Jungleland, an entertainment area featuring the exhibition of animals, both wild and tame. Peter Hale, owner of Jungleland, is married to Julie. His first wife, Lisa, was killed by a leopard as she performed her world-famous act. Hale is devoted to his first wife's memory and determined to kill Philip Tager who caused her death. He knows that his first wife had fallen in love with Tager, that Tager had led her on to a point where she was ready to leave her husband, then told her that he would never marry her. Before Lisa entered the performing cage, she dug a pin into the leopard's paw. The enraged beast killed her. Hale knows Lisa committed suicide.

Hale has kept the leopard who killed Lisa. He is determined that Tager die in the same manner as she did. He invites Tager to the unveiling of a memorial to Lisa. Meanwhile, Julie, who loves Hale, has learned of his plans. She pleads with Tod to stay close to Tager. Hale gets Tager drunk, and then carries him into the cage where the wild animals perform. Hale is about to open the door to let the leopard into the cage when Lisa stops him. She makes him realize that if he pursues this murderous revenge, they can never find happiness together. Tod leaves Hale and Julie whose love has conquered his hate.

Cast: Tod (*Martin Milner*), Peter Hale (*Peter Graves*), Julie (*Eva Stern*), Brauner (*Charles H. Radilac*), Philip Tager (*Michael Pate*), Wasson (*Henry Beckman*).

#62. From an Enchantress Fleeing

Executive Producer: **H. B. Leonard**
Written by: **Stirling Silliphant**
Directed by: **William A. Graham**

Dr. Lawrence Martin is an inventor of electronic robots. He has retreated to the world of the laboratory—far from the social sphere of success so much admired by his daughter Lorrie and his wife Anna. Anna, to whom worldly success means more than anything else, has worked up an enormously successful dental practice. Tod gets a job assisting her. He helps to conceal from her young patients the realistic aspects of dental treatment. Anna gives a big party to bring her husband into her own social climate. He runs away and joins a group of other men who are refugees from their wives' insatiable compulsion for success.

Lawrence starts working on a machine which will recreate the courting stage in every young couple's life. He proves that such a machine—by choosing the proper perfume, music, romantic setting—could win the heart of any young girl. He tries out the machine, but the fiancée of the girl whose responses he is testing, destroys it. Lawrence runs away to a small town where he makes chairs by hand. Tod finds him. He realizes that Lawrence and his wife miss each other. By showing Anna the false environment in which she lives, he gets her to rejoin Lawrence.

Cast: Tod (*Martin Milner*), Dr. Lawrence Martin (*Arthur O'Connell*), Lorrie (*Anne Helm*), Dr. Anna Martin (*June Vincent*), Gunther (*Milton Seltzer*), Ames (*Biff Elliot*).

ROUTE 66 – THIRD SEASON

	Episode Title	Air Date
63.	One Tiger to a Hill	9/21/62
64.	Journey to Nineveh	9/28/62
65.	Man Out of Time	10/5/62
66.	Ever Ride the Waves in Oklahoma?	10/12/62
67.	Voice at the End of the Line	10/19/62
68.	Lizard's Leg and Owlet's Wing	10/26/62
69.	Across Walnuts and Wine	11/2/62
70.	Welcome to the Wedding	11/9/62
71.	Every Father's Daughter Must Weave Her Own	11/16/62
72.	Poor Little Kangaroo Rat	11/23/62
73.	Hey Moth, Come Eat the Flame	11/30/62
74.	Only by Cunning Glimpses	12/7/62
75.	Where is Chick Lorimer? Where Has She Gone?	12/14/62
76.	Give an Old Cat a Tender Mouse	12/21/62
77.	A Bunch of Lonely Pagliaccis	1/4/63
78.	You Can't Pick Cotton in Tahiti	1/11/63
79.	A Gift for a Warrior	1/18/63
80.	Suppose I said I was the Queen of Spain	2/8/63
81.	Somehow It Gets to Be Tomorrow	2/15/63
82.	Shall Forfeit His Dog and Ten Shillings to the King	2/22/63
83.	In the Closing of a Trunk	3/8/63
84.	The Cage Around Maria	3/15/63
85.	Fifty Miles from Home	3/22/63
86.	Narcissus on an Old Red Fire Engine	3/29/63
87.	The Cruelest Sea of All	4/5/63
88.	Peace, Pity, Pardon	4/12/63
89.	What a Shining Young Man Was Our Gallant Lieutenant	4/26/63
90.	But What Do You Do in March?	5/3/63
91.	Who Will Cheer My Bonnie Bride?	5/10/63
92.	Shadows of an Afternoon	5/17/63
93.	Soda Pop and Paper Flags	5/24/63

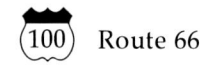

#63. One Tiger to a Hill

Executive Producer: **H. B. Leonard**
Written by: **Stirling Silliphant**
Directed by: **David Lowell Rich**

Tod and Buz are working on a salmon fishing boat in Astoria, Oregon. When Tod shows an interest in Toika, their employer's daughter, a jealous fisherman named Karno confronts Tod on the pier and starts a fight. Tod prevails but Karno proves relentless. When Karno cuts their fishing lines and takes a shot at them, Buz goes after him.

Karno refuses to be taunted into a fight by Buz. Later, he reveals to Tod his belief that the world is an evil and malevolent jungle. Karno tells Tod that his own inability to shoot an unarmed German prisoner during the war led to the massacre of his entire unit. Karno's disgust and repulsion of life resulted from this experience. Although Karno has confessed the belief which motivates his actions, he doesn't let up on Tod, and continues to threaten him.

Karno abducts Toika on his boat, and Tod follows. Karno batters Tod. Tod's answering blows force Karno overboard, and all feel he has drowned. Tod is unable to comprehend Karno's intense hatred, and feels despondent.

Later, Karno is rescued. He reveals that his brush with death has finally taught him the true values of life.

Cast: Tod (*Martin Milner*), Buz (*George Maharis*), Karno (*David Janssen*), Anna Gustafson (*Signe Hasso*), Toika (*Laura Devon*).

#64. Journey to Nineveh

Executive Producer: **H. B. Leonard**
Written by: **William R. Cox**
Directed by: **David Lowell Rich**

Tod and Buz meet Jonah Butler in the small town of Harleyville, where they decide to spend a day fishing. Jonah's neighbors consider him a jinx. Jonah believes it himself. Tod and Buz start to share the belief when a series of unfortunate happenings, including a dunking in the lake, occur while fishing with Jonah.

Meanwhile back at Jonah's hometown, Sam, his older brother, has purchased a truck for $50. Then Frank Lauterbach, the Constable's son, demands that Suzy Butler, Sam's granddaughter, return a cheap ring. Since Suzy put the ring in the tackle box which Jonah has with him, she is unable to do so. Claiming Sam sold the ring to buy the truck, Frank has him arrested.

Buz cures Jonah of the belief that he is a jinx, and Jonah catches one of the largest fish ever seen in the vicinity.

Producing the ring in court, Jonah has the case against his brother dismissed. Frank and two tough friends start to wreck Sam's truck. Tod and Buz take them on. Badly beaten, the vicious trio flee. Tod and Buz, Jonah and Suzy, joyously join in celebrating Sam's birthday.

Cast: Tod (*Martin Milner*), Buz (*George Maharis*), Sam Butler (*Joe E. Brown*), Jonah Butler (*Buster Keaton*), Suzy Butler (*Jenny Maxwell*), Constable (*Guy Raymond*), Gas Attendant (*John Astin*), Abe (*Edgar Buchanan*), Frank (*John Davis Chandler*), Charlie (*John Durren*), Woman Driver (*Virginia Rose*), Jake (*Russell Horton*).

#65. Man Out of Time

Executive Producer: **H. B. Leonard**
Written by: **Larry Marcus**
Directed by: **David Lowell Rich**

Buz and Tod are driving cabs in Chicago when Harry Wender, a former gangster, who has spent the last thirty-two years in prison, returns to the big town. Tod saves Harry's life, flinging him away from the path of a freight truck. Harry is sure that some enemy from his past is trying to kill him. Tod feels compassion for the old man. Tod and Buz, each working different shifts, are hired by Harry. Harry tells them that he has received a threatening phone call. Harry insists on searching for the person he feels is trying to kill him, and refuses police protection.

Old Sandy Leeds, once a top newspaper man, gives Harry a line on the survivors from his past who might have reason for killing him. All names are checked out—they are either dead, or have completely forgotten the past. Finally, Harry finds Laverne, whose life he ruined. Harry breaks down when he learns Laverne has forgiven him. Finally, he finds the driver he thought had tried to crush him with the freight truck, has been trailing him to ask that charges be dropped, as he might lose his job because of carelessness.

Tod and Buz realize the threatening phone calls have been in Harry's mind, which has broken, and they arrange for him to be taken to the County Hospital.

Cast: Tod (*Martin Milner*), Buz (*George Maharis*), Harry Wender (*Luther Adler*), Sandy (*Frank McHugh*), Jake (*Bruce Gordon*), Laverne (*Glenda Farrell*).

#66. Ever Ride the Waves in Oklahoma?

Executive Producer: **Herbert B. Leonard**
Written by: **Stirling Silliphant**
Directed by: **Robert Gist**

In Huntington Beach, California, Tod and Buz give a ride to young Jimmy Mills, a surfboard rider. Jimmy is on his way to challenge Hob Harrell, king of the beach, in "shooting the pier," by mounting a surfboard, catching a wave, and riding it through the pilings. Jimmy tries, hits the pilings, and dies. Buz becomes incensed over Hob's casual attitude toward this waste of life. Buz decks Hob and is restrained by his entourage. Hob refuses to brawl. Buz vows to bring him down somehow.

Debbie, a beautiful surfboard rider, offers to teach Buz to ride so he can challenge Hob. Buz becomes proficient and tries to "shoot the pier." He slips off his surfboard just as it smashes into a piling. Still angry with the entire surf-riding crowd, Buz humiliates Hob in front of his admirers by revealing that "the king" works as a night time bus boy in a local restaurant.

Tod is disgusted by Buz's actions. Buz and Hob brawl, and Buz beats Hob, but he feels no satisfaction from his victory. Buz publicly admits Hob's superiority and his own failure. The next morning, before dawn, he goes out alone and "shoots the pier."

Cast: Tod (*Martin Milner*), Buz (*George Maharis*), Hob (*Jeremy Slate*), Debbie (*Romney Tree*), Jimmy (*Bruce Watson*), First Surfer (*Ron Kipling*), Second Surfer (*Rad Fulton*), Waiter (*Tony DeMarco*), Medrith (*Dolores Michaels*).

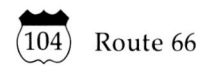

#67. Voice at the End of the Line

Executive Producer: **H. B. Leonard**
Written by: **Larry Marcus**
Directed by: **David Lowell Rich**

On the first day at his new job, Buz becomes the unsuspecting accomplice in a practical joke on Sam, a co-worker. Led by Jack, a nasty stock clerk, the men bug the phone on Sam's phone calls to Ruthie. Sam is pretending to be young, handsome and debonair. His private conversation is broadcast over a loudspeaker. Feeling remorse for what he had done, Buz intervenes as Jack and his co-workers taunt Sam. Jack swings at Buz, and pays the price. Buz reaches out to Sam who runs away totally humiliated. As revenge, Jack calls Ruthie and tells her the truth about Sam; then he hides in the shadows and slugs Buz with a heavy club.

Sam, terribly embarrassed, quits his job and moves out of his rooming house. Buz feels responsible for Sam's unhappiness and searches for him. Buz convinces Sam not to leave Chicago, and hatches a wild scheme: Tod will impersonate Sam in a meeting with Ruthie. Ruthie will think Sam is handsome, and then the relationship can continue over the phone as before. A young, pretty Ruthie appears at the meeting and Tod falls for her. Tod searches for Ruthie. When he finds her, he realizes that she is not Ruthie and that Ruthie, also self-conscious about the image she presents to the world, has also gotten a stand-in. Tod and Buz force Sam to meet Ruthie—the real Ruthie and the boys leave them together.

Cast: Tod (*Martin Milner*), Buz (*George Maharis*), Sam Frazier (*Sorrell Booke*), Jack (*Frank Campanella*), Ruthie (*Marsha Greenhouse*), Mr. Morgenstern (*Lou Gilbert*), Roy (*Peter Gumeny*), Charlie (*Mike Dana*).

#68. Lizard's Leg and Owlet's Wing

Executive Producer: **H. B. Leonard**
Written by: **Stirling Silliphant**
Directed by: **Robert Gist**

Tod and Buz are hired as convention coordinators by the O'Hare Inn in Chicago. Buz winds up shepherding a convention of beautiful executive secretaries. Tod finds himself acting as coordinator for Boris Karloff, Peter Lorre and Lon Chaney, Jr., who are meeting to discuss the feasibility of a TV series based on their old horror movies. Lorre and Chaney find it difficult to convince Karloff—who thinks horror is a thing of the past—it still is a great entertainment attraction.

Buz bars Tod from mingling with the beautiful secretaries. Tod starts scheming for revenge. He persuades Lorre to try a scare test on the girls to prove his point to Karloff. Shrieking and fainting secretaries dot the inn, when Chaney goes into his act as the Wolfman.

Meanwhile, Karloff has been sympathetic to Molly Cross, immersed in her unrequited love for her boss. Chaney tries to frighten her. Molly's love prevents her from feeling fear, and she shows compassion for him. However, Karloff, after stopping to bring Molly and her boss together, is convinced by the reaction of the other girls. Amazed by the ingenuity of Tod's revenge, Buz agrees to split up the remaining secretaries with him.

Cast: Tod (*Martin Milner*), Buz (*George Maharis*), Peter Lorre (*Himself*), Lon Chaney, Jr., (*Himself*), Boris Karloff (*Himself*), Mr. Paris (*Conrad Nagel*), Mrs. Baxter (*Martita Hunt*), Molly Cross (*Jeannine Riley*).

#69. Across Walnuts & Wine

Executive Producer: **Herbert B. Leonard**
Written by: **Stirling Silliphant**
Directed by: **Herbert B. Leonard**

Buz and Tod come to Maggie Ely's house in Oregon City, Oregon to board while working at a local lumber mill. Immediately, they feel the tensions in the house. Autumn, Maggie's older sister, has just arrived for what looks like a long, and not entirely welcome, visit. Maggie herself makes a little extra household money by conducting séances, and her husband Van putters in his garage workshop on meaningless inventions. Their nephew, Mike, a nasty young man, threatens Maggie and Van with eviction when he becomes twenty-one and inherits title to the house. Most of Mike's day is spent trying to avoid the five Kranz brothers, who are after him for his treatment of their sister.

Buz and Tod are embarrassed being in the middle of so much waste and unhappiness, but decide to stick it out for a week. As tensions build, Maggie deliberately destroys a near-completed invention of Van's so that he will at least have his dreams remaining. The Kranz brothers take up position in front of the house, determined to wait until Mike comes out. Finally, Autumn cracks. She admits to Mike that she was fired from her job as school teacher because she had no love to give to her school children, and that she came to their house for a place to hide. Mike realizes his errors, tears up the eviction notice, and goes out to face the Kranz brothers.

Cast: Tod (*Martin Milner*), Buz (*George Maharis*), Autumn Ely (*Nina Foch*), Maggie Carter (*Betty Field*), Van Carter (*James Dunn*), Michael Ely (*Robert Walker*), Waldo (*Dick Thies*), Corinne Carter (*Sindee Anna Richards*).

#70. Welcome to the Wedding

Executive Producer: **H. B. Leonard**
Written by: **Howard Rodman**
Directed by: **George Sherman**

In Portland, Oregon, Buz and Tod have been asked to usher at a friend's wedding. Tod goes to the train station to await the arrival of his date. There, Tod meets Peers, a policeman, and Justin Lezama, his prisoner. Peers tells Tod that Lezama's brother, Stanley, lives in town. The policeman adds that the brothers haven't seen each other in years. Although unwilling, Tod finally agrees to get Stanley so the brothers can meet, possibly for the last time. Tod brings Stanley back. Stanley pulls a gun, shoots the policeman, but is himself wounded.

Lezama frees himself while holding a gun on Tod, and then cold-bloodedly kills his wounded brother. After handcuffing Tod to the wheel of a car, Lezama drives around Portland digging up $100,000 he had hidden before his arrest. Lezama explains to Tod that he feels no emotion, no guilt for his killings.

Lezama demands that Tod take him to the wedding. He threatens to kill a child at random if Tod refuses. At the wedding, Lezama abducts Tod and his date, and forces them to go with him to Stanley's home. Buz arrives with the police and Lezama opens fire. The policemen kill Lezama. Tod and Buz return to the wedding.

Cast: Tod (*Martin Milner*), Buz (*George Maharis*), Lezama (*Rod Steiger*), Custody Officer Peers (*Edward Asner*), Stanley (*David Clarke*).

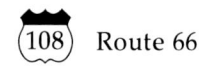

#71. Every Father's Daughter Must Weave Her Own

Executive Producer: **H. B. Leonard**
Written by: **Anthony Lawrence**
Directed by: **Richard L. Bare**

Near Chicago, Buz and Tod are employed in the construction of highways by John Rados. John Rados, in his late fifties, is a self-made man. He has two children, Nick and Ara. Buz and Tod are immediately impressed by Ara's beauty. Rados notices Ara's interest in Buz and Tod. Rados surprises Buz and Tod by asking them to show Ara a good time. He tells them that he broke up an affair which was not good for her and she hasn't forgiven him. Nick warns his father not to degrade Ara. Of course, Buz and Ara find a mutual interest without the help of Rados. Nick, feeling Buz has accepted his father's offer, warns him to keep away from Ara. While dancing with Buz, Ara's face contorts with pain and she runs away.

Nick finally breaks down and tells Buz that Ara is dying. Buz demands that Rados reveal the truth to Ara. Rados tells Buz that his wife died of the same disease and he couldn't bear seeing the same reaction to the approach of death. Finally, Rados discovers that Ara has learned the truth herself. However, he unwittingly reveals that he has tried to buy Buz to show affection for Ara. Stricken because she believed Buz actually loved her, Ara runs away. Buz follows. Although at first she spurns him, Ara finally listens and realizes that she can find once more the true values which have always given meaning to her life.

Cast: Tod (*Martin Milner*), Buz (*George Maharis*), Ara Rados (*Madlyn Rhue*), John Rados (*Jack Kruschen*), Nick Rados (*Robert Drivas*).

#72. Poor Little Kangaroo Rat

Executive Producer: **Herbert B. Leonard**
Written by: **Les Pine**
Directed by: **Walter E. Grauman**

In California, Doctor Duncan employs Buz and Tod to fish for sharks for his experiments. Duncan, aided by his lovely assistant Liz Penfold, is using the liver of the sharks for basic research on cholesterol. After four years, the experiments have been entirely unsuccessful. Doc's wife, Helen, is set against the project. Liz's feelings for Doc go beyond professional admiration.

Helen explains to Tod that she feels her husband has an obligation to her and their son, Chet, to provide for them financially rather than waste his talents on this project. She wants him to give up basic research and enter medical practice. Doc refuses to do this. Helen decides to leave Doc and take Chet with her. Tod tries to give her some of the money he and Buz have saved, to make it possible for her to stay on, but she refuses.

Doc is hurt by her defection, and begins drinking. When his latest experiment ends in failure, Doc goes berserk, and destroys all his live sharks. Feeling remorseful, Doc is willing to give up his research, but Helen, with Buz's help, realizes its importance to him, and stays on.

Cast: Tod (*Martin Milner*), Buz (*George Maharis*), Doc Duncan (*Leslie Nielsen*), Helen (*Joanne Linville*), Liz (*Maggie Pierce*), Chet (*Ronny Howard*).

#73. Hey Moth, Come Eat the Flame

Executive Producer: **H. B. Leonard**
Written by: **Stirling Silliphant**
Directed by: **James Sheldon**

Employed in a quarry, Tod and Buz find lodgings in a boarding house in nearby St. Louis, Missouri. Muddy Mullins, an alcoholic, who plays piano in a local night spot, rooms with his fifteen year old son, Arnie, across the hall. Having visited his father while he was serving time, Arnie finds it impossible to show any real affection for him. Tod and Buz are unsuccessful in their efforts to help Arnie, who practically carries his father home every night. Muddy, who feels that he can win his son's affection if he improves their living standards, accepts the offer of Hannibal, a top mobster, to drive the getaway car in a planned holdup of a factory.

Buz finally gets through to Arnie and takes him to a meeting of young teenagers whose parents are alcoholics. Although Buz feels that meeting with teenagers who have a similar problem will help Arnie, it has the opposite result. Arnie runs away. Tod, searching for Muddy, makes his way to a garage where he has been told he can find him. Muddy has just informed Hannibal that he can't go through with the robbery. Tod's arrival stops Hannibal from beating Muddy. Meanwhile, Arnie has climbed to a high ledge of the quarry and is about to jump. Tod and Muddy arrive as Buz is trying to save him. Muddy, brushing Tod and Buz aside, wins his son's respect by rescuing him himself.

Cast: Tod (*Martin Milner*), Buz (*George Maharis*), Muddy Mullins (*Harry Guardino*), Hannibal (*Mike Kellin*), Arnie Mullins (*Mickey Sholdar*), Janic (*Jennifer Billingsley*).

#74. Only by Cunning Glimpses

Executive Producer: **H. B. Leonard**
Written by: **Stirling Silliphant**
Directed by: **Tom Gries**

In Cleveland, Tod and Buz attend a performance given by Brycie Koseloff, a mind reader. Brycie's father, Dr. Anton Koseloff, is in the audience. Whereas Brycie claims to be able to look into the future, Dr. Koseloff spends his life debunking the claims of spiritualists, since he believes the future is closed to everyone. To impress her father, Brycie claims she sees something terrible happening to Tod. Tod and Buz go to Brycie's dressing room. As Dr. Koseloff tries to convince Tod and Buz that she can't predict the fate of others, Brycie tells Tod that he will kill Buz.

Buz tries to convince Tod that there is nothing to Brycie's predictions. Tod, gripped in the clutch of the unknown, feels he will harm Buz in some manner, particularly since incidents which Brycie claimed would lead up to the killing, seem to happen. Meanwhile, Dr. Koseloff is cooperating with the police in breaking up a phony séance ring, which meets in a barn. Driving through a storm, Tod and Buz arrive at the barn just as it breaks into flames. Tod, feeling that Buz will die in the fire as proof of Brycie's prediction, fights to keep Buz from rushing into the barn to save those who have been trapped. Buz and Tod are brought together once more when Brycie tells Tod that she lied to him and that she can't see into the future.

Cast: Tod (*Martin Milner*), Buz (*George Maharis*), Dr. Anton Koseloff (*Theodore Bikel*), Brycie Koseloff (*Lois Smith*).

Route 66

#75. Where is Chick Lorimer? Where Has She Gone?

Executive Producer: **H. B. Leonard**
Written by: **Larry Marcus**
Directed by: **George Sherman**

In Missouri, Ellen Barnes, a stripteaser, fast-talks Tod into helping her escape from Jack Harris, a bail bondsman. Then, slamming the door of her car on Tod's fingers, she drives away. Tod, learning that she owes Harris $2,000 bail money, feels he has misjudged him. Tod follows Ellen to St. Charles, Missouri, her hometown, where her relatives and neighbors know nothing about her profession. There Ellen is presiding over the wedding of her niece, Jeannie O'Brien to Ralph.

Ellen meets Peter Graham, a former suitor. Ellen feels she can find redemption from her past, but sees Graham run away. Emotionally touched by Ellen, Tod approaches and promises to keep her secret. Secure in Tod's promise, Ellen returns to her family, still feeling she can find a place in the life she once knew. However, Harris appears and exposes the life she thought she had left behind. Shamed, Ellen runs away to a cemetery. Tod follows and tries to convince Ellen that they could find happiness together. Deeply touched, Ellen refuses and leaves town.

Cast: Tod (*Martin Milner*), Ellen Barnes (*Vera Miles*), Ruth O'Brien (*Martha Scott*), Peter Graham (*Frank Overton*), Jackson Harris (*Robert Emhardt*).

Third Season

#76. Give an Old Cat a Tender Mouse

Executive Producer: **H. B. Leonard**
Written by: **Stirling Silliphant**
Directed by: **Tom Gries**

Vickie Russell, the beautiful blond whom Tod and Buz once met in Tucson, passes Tod on her motorcycle as he is entering Memphis. Vickie's cycle is being followed by a Highway Cruiser, driven by Pogo Popkin, a detective hired by the trustee of Vickie's large estate, to follow and keep her out of trouble. Tod, recognizing Vickie, speeds after her, only to be stopped by a traffic policeman.

Vickie enters the Cotton Exchange. She asks for Frank Bridenbaugh, wealthy scion of a southern cotton family, whom the trustees have suggested as a fitting match for her. As they talk, Frank begins falling in love with her.

Vickie finds Frank's ordered existence repugnant, but his skill and excitement in sky-diving intrigues her. She meets his family and friends at a society ball, after which she drags him to her milieu—a downtown jazz club. Frank is out of his element and swings at a man he finds talking to Vickie. Tod arrives just in time to take one punch and get himself arrested—by the same cop. Vickie gives it one more chance the next day. However, when Frank finds she rides a horse better than he can, he resigns from what he feels will be a constant test of strength. Vickie heads out of town. Tod follows until he is arrested again—by the same cop.

Cast: Tod (*Martin Milner*), Vickie (*Julie Newmar*), Frank Bridenbaugh (*Robert Webber*), Emily Bridenbaugh (*Natalie Schafer*).

#77. A Bunch of Lonely Pagliaccis

Executive Producer: **H. B. Leonard**
Written by: **Stirling Silliphant**
Directed by: **Tom Gries**

In Tennessee, Warren Barr, world family novelist, hires Tod to perform a gamut of assignments from researcher to chauffeur. Barr's daughter, Mrs. Beth Chance, shoots her husband, Larry, when she finds him with Cora Parkes. Soon newspapermen and members of every other media profession descend upon the town to cover the story. Even though Barr hires a top attorney to defend his daughter, she refuses to give any reason for her action. Meanwhile, Cora has been taken to a hiding place until the trial. Certain that Cora is the key to the case, Tod searches for her and finally finds her. He brings Warren to Cora. Cora, claiming to be certain that Beth won't be convicted, refuses to talk further with Warren.

Beth confesses to her father how much she loved Larry and now she feels alone. Finally, Beth, in a meeting with Tod in her cell, tells him she must speak the truth—she can't allow Larry to be defiled any longer. She asks him to tell this to Cora. Cora comes to see Warren. She tells him that Beth and she knew Larry was dying from a painful and incurable disease. They had set up the seemingly sordid scene so Beth could save Larry from further suffering, and have grounds for acquittal. After this unexpected development, Beth is found guilty with a recommendation for clemency. Tod drives Barr home.

Cast: Tod (*Martin Milner*), Warren Barr (*Barry Sullivan*), Leslie Stone (*Warren Stevens*), Beth (*Vivian Blaine*), Jimmy Russell (*James Leo Herlihy*), Cora Parkes (*Mary Munday*).

#78. You Can't Pick Cotton in Tahiti

Executive Producer: **H. B. Leonard**
Written by: **Shimon Wincelberg**
Directed by: **Robert Ellis Miller**

Faking suicide, Julian Roebuck, who has managed to elude all normal involvements, escapes marriage in Hollywood and boards a bus. The bus stops at Lake Chisholm, Tennessee, where Tod is working in a cotton gin. Julian sees Elva Dupree, a country beauty, and immediately inquires about hotel accommodations. Elva's boyfriend, Skeeter, starts to fume when Elva, hypnotized, invites him to stay with her folks.

Julian hears some of the natives singing folk songs. Excited by the possibility of a new career, he starts recording the singing. Julian, a kiss-and-run type, finds Elva has fallen in love with him. He tries to fend her off. Mrs. Dupree tells Julian he must leave because of the effect he is having on Elva. Determined to finish his opus based on folk music, Julian promises to marry Elva when he has completed his work.

After recording the last note, Julian tries to sneak out of town. Skeeter and the Duprees bar his departure, and he is kept prisoner in the Dupree home. Although Tod excoriates Julian for his inhuman treatment of people, he agrees to help him escape. Skeeter and his friends are waiting. Julian eludes his pursuers, and places another fake suicide note near a lake. Elva returns to Skeeter, and the town to normal. Later, driving away from Lake Chisholm, Tod sees a hitchhiker ahead. It is Julian. Tod drives past him.

Cast: Tod (*Martin Milner*), Julian Roebuck (*Richard Basehart*), Elva (*Jena Engstrom*), Skeeter (*William Barmlette*), Mr. Dupree (*Richard Shannon*), Mrs. Dupree (*Adrienne Marden*), Pappy French (*Pat Malone*).

#79. A Gift for a Warrior

Executive Producer: **H. B. Leonard**
Written by: **Larry Marcus**
Directed by: **David Lowell Rich**

Tod and Buz pick up Eric, a young German, who has deserted a freighter at San Diego. Eric tells them he has come to find his father, Ralph Vincent, an ex-GI. After Eric leaves them, Tod and Buz find evidence leading them to believe Eric plans to kill Ralph. Tod and Buz drive to Ralph's farm. Eric admits he has come to kill Ralph who he believes deserted his dead mother. Norma, Ralph's young wife, driven by some hidden discontent, plays up to Eric. Eric feels he has found a way to destroy Ralph.

Eric leads Ralph to believe that Norma has run away with him. Ralph shows Tod a picture of Eric's mother. He relates that he did everything possible to find her, but was told she was dead. Ralph learns Eric is his son and finds him with Norma. Norma swears nothing has happened, but Ralph runs away and drops dead of a heart attack.

Eric learns of Ralph's long search for his mother. Norma tells Eric that her bitterness stems from the fact that Ralph married her because she reminded him of his long lost love. Tod and Buz feel the horror that will be part of Eric for the rest of his life.

Cast: Tod (*Martin Milner*), Buz (*George Maharis*), Ralph (*James Whitmore*), Norma (*Carolyn Kearney*), Eric (*Lars Passgard*).

#80. Suppose I Said I Was the Queen of Spain

Executive Producer: **H. B. Leonard**
Written by: **Stirling Silliphant**
Directed by: **David Lowell Rich**

In California, Tod meets a beautiful girl. He realizes she has been following him for some time. When she refuses to give him her name, he decides to call her Isabel. A romance ensues. Then "Isabel" disappears, and Tod finds his credit card is missing. He learns that over $9,000 worth of purchases have been made with it. Tod searches for the girl and finds her working at a welfare mission. She disclaims being "Isabel" and identifies herself as Susan Ames. Trying to get at the root of the mystery, Tod has the girl taken to police headquarters. The police release her. An official of the credit company tells Tod that everything purchased on his credit card has been returned. More than ever, Tod determines to see the girl again.

Tod goes to the mission, and finds she has left there. Tod is about to give up the search when he receives a phone call from the girl to meet her at a university campus. Now calling herself Lila, the girl pretends this is a chance meeting. She tells Tod she is a student in the drama school at the university. She asks him to listen to a play she is writing as part of the course. They go to an empty auditorium. The girl recites the lines from her play. Tod sadly realizes that his part in her life has been a creation of her fantasy, to be the necessary foil to one of the many characterizations she would create for herself before, if ever, she found her own role in life.

Cast: Tod (*Martin Milner*), Isabel (*Lois Nettleton*), Lee (*Robert Duvall*), Lieutenant Cook (*Philip Abbott*).

#81. Somehow It Gets To Be Tomorrow

Executive Producer: **H. B. Leonard**
Written by: **Stirling Silliphant**
Directed by: **David Lowell Rich**

Joby Paxton, thirteen, steals the new club house funds of a young men's tennis association. Pursued by the members, Joby leaps into Tod's car, and pleads with Tod to save him. When police stop the car, Joby disappears. Later, Ebin Corelli, a welfare department caseworker, comes to see Tod. He tells Tod that Joby and his eight-year-old sister, Susie, were orphaned when their parents were drowned.

The welfare department picked Mr. and Mrs. Conwell as foster parents for Joby and his sister, but the children's love for their own parents was so strong that they could not adjust to the change. Joby, who idolized his father, has run away from the Conwells, hoping to find someone he could respect as much as his father. Corelli feels that Joby is testing Tod, but asks Tod to help him catch Joby. Little by little, Joby uses every possible method to test Tod, even involving him in a fight to judge his fighting prowess.

Joby, finally feeling he has found someone he can trust, tells Tod of his plans to run away with his sister. Although Tod agrees to help the children, he is torn because he knows he must betray them to Corelli. Driving the children to a bus station, Tod reveals his perfidy. Before Corelli arrives, the heartbroken children run away.

Cast: Tod (*Martin Milner*), Corelli (*Martin Balsam*), Joby (*Roger Mobley*), Susie (*Leslye Hunter*), Mr. Conwell (*Bill Southern*), Mrs. Conwell (*Dell Aldrich*), Auctioneer (*G. K. Stubbs*).

#82. Shall Forfeit His Dog and Ten Shillings to the King

Executive Producer: **H. B. Leonard**
Written by: **Stirling Silliphant**
Directed by: **Tom Gries**

Two holdup men, Babe and Landers, rob and kill the owner of an Arizona trailer community for senior citizens where Tod is employed. Tod joins a posse, headed by Hank Saxon, to track the killers to Superstition Mountain. Included in the posse are General Scranton, an old Army man, who insists, despite opposition because of his age, on joining the posse, and his wife Diana Kirk.

Saxon leads Diana to a spot where he has sighted Landers. Saxon shoots and kills Landers after Diana falters, but gives Diana credit for the killing. Tod and General Scranton trap Babe. Babe tells them that the holdup was planned by Saxon who then double-crossed his two confederates, expecting to keep the stolen money for himself, as well as getting Diana to marry him. Shortly after this disclosure, Saxon arrives on the scene and shoots Babe. Wily old General Scranton, in a death-paced gun duel, kills Saxon.

Mounting his horse, Tod follows the survivor of the senseless killing back to town.

Cast: Tod (*Martin Milner*), Hank Saxon (*Steve Cochran*), Diana Kirk (*Kathleen Crowley*), Terry (*Med Flory*), Babe (*L. Q. Jones*), General Scranton (*John Anderson*), Sheriff Haskell (*James Brown*), Landers (*Gary Cockrell*).

#83. In the Closing of a Trunk

Executive Producer: **H. B. Leonard**
Written by: **Stirling Silliphant**
Directed by: **Ralph Senensky**

For twenty-seven years, Kyle Hawkes has nourished a hatred for his niece, Alma Hawkes, who murdered her father—his brother. Shortly after Hawkes gives Tod a job on his ferry boat, Alma returns to Corpus Christi, from prison, determined to find her son. Hawkes has raised the boy, Mattie, protected him from the shame of his illegitimate birth, and also taught him to hate his mother. Hawkes finds that Alma feels that Tod may be her son. Still driven by the desire for revenge, and determined to keep Mattie from her, Hawkes plays upon both Alma and Tod, until she actually believes Tod is her son.

Tod is completely disgusted when he realizes how he has been used and fights with Mattie. Later, Mattie makes an effort to convince Alma he is her son, but she is sure he is trying to replace Tod. Tod realizes he must leave. Before he does so, he makes one last effort to prove to Alma that he is not her son.

While he is there, Kyle sends the trunk in which Alma had placed her father's dead body years before. Alma's mind breaks under the impact. She confuses Tod with her father. Tod tries to escape her fury. He trips, strikes his head, and is knocked unconscious. Alma puts him in the trunk. She rushes to tell Kyle. After saving Tod, Kyle finally realizes his brother was a brutal father, and that Alma killed him to save her baby. Later, when Alma is taken away in an ambulance, Mattie sits beside his mother.

Cast: Tod (*Martin Milner*), Kyle Hawkes (*Ed Begley*), Alma Hawkes (*Ruth Roman*), Mattie (*Don Dubbins*), Arty (*Guy Raymond*).

#84. The Cage Around Maria

Executive Producer: **H. B. Leonard**
Written by: **Jesse Sandler**
Directed by: **George Sherman**

Tod gets a job as tour conductor at the Houston Zoo. One day Maria Cardenas, nineteen, enters the bear grotto. Tod rescues her. Although Maria refuses to give him any reasons for her act, Tod drives her home. There Tod meets her stepfather, Juan Pablo De Amundo. Juan gives riding lessons on the huge estate. Maria introduces him as a stable boy whom her mother married after Maria's father died. Elena, her mother, is a semi-invalid since the cinch strap of her saddle broke six months before. She walks with a cane. Maria, telling Tod that Juan tried to make love to her, gets him to believe that Juan is trying to kill her mother.

Tod has a long talk with Elena. Elena feels that Maria refuses to accept Juan because she idolized her father. She tells Tod that she loves Juan and is certain that he loves her. Then Elena falls down a flight of stairs, her cane having been cut almost in two. For the first time, Elena feels Juan may be trying to kill her. Tod meets Juan. Juan tells Tod he is leaving. Juan tells Tod that he did not try to kill Elena, whom he loves.

Maria appears with a gun, determined to shoot Juan, because she believes he is trying to kill her mother in order to get possession of the family fortune. Juan tells her their only money comes from his riding lessons. Maria, unable to pull the trigger, admits she loves Juan. Maria runs away and drives to the bear pit. Tod and Juan follow. They finally catch the girl who, caught in the bars of her madness, has almost brought tragedy to all.

Cast: Tod (*Martin Milner*), Maria (*Elizabeth Ashley*), Juan De Amundo (*Mario Alcalde*), Elena De Amundo (*Beatrice Straight*), Dr. Burton (*Peter Brocco*).

#85. Fifty Miles From Home

Executive Producer: **H. B. Leonard**
Written by: **Stirling Silliphant**
Directed by: **James Sheldon**

Private First Class Lincoln (Linc) Case, a hero of the Vietnam struggle, arrives in Houston aboard a bus. Willow, who has fallen in love with Case, follows him. Linc is trying to brush the girl off. His actions are resented by a group of college basketball players whom Tod has been coaching. He offers no resistance when they start pushing him around. However, when they trip him, he falls and gashes his forehead. Then Linc explodes. Using ju jitsu and karate, Linc mercilessly wades into the group, sending most to the hospital and maiming one for life.

After Linc goes to the hospital to see Robbie, one of the boys, he leaves for his home town where a hero's welcome awaits him. Willow and Tod drive after him. Tod finally catches up with Linc. In the fight that follows, Linc eschews the brutal methods he had perfected in combat. Fighting to a draw, Linc and Tod come to respect each other.

Linc asks Tod for a lift back to Houston after he has seen his mother. Willow finally realizes that although they may come together in the future, there is no place for her at the present in Linc's life. Linc's mother pleads with him to stay for the celebration which will mean so much to his father. Linc tells his mother about the Vietnamese family who sacrificed their lives to save his. He tells her he hopes to return home, but first must find himself. Linc drives away from town with Tod.

Cast: Tod (*Martin Milner*), Linc Case (*Glenn Corbett*), Willow (*Susan Oliver*), Mr. Beale (*Robert Emhardt*), Mrs. Case (*Linda Watkins*), Robbie Beale (*Berkeley Harris*).

#86. Narcissus on an Old Red Fire Engine

Executive Producer: **Herbert B. Leonard**
Written by: **Joel Carpenter**
Directed by: **Ralph Senensky**

Tod Stiles and Lincoln Case are employed by a cotton compressing company in Galveston. In a small bar frequented by Greek merchant seamen, Linc meets Janie, a beautiful young girl who has retreated into a world of her own. Paul and Nick, Janie's friends, resent Linc's appraisal of Janie and put a "Mickey" in his beer. However, Linc falls for Janie and she plays along with him, hoping he will be her key to the real world. Pleas by the Chief of Police, a friend of Janie's family, that Linc keep away from Janie have no effect on him.

Tod and Linc meet with Janie's parents, Mr. and Mrs. Nickerson, after the Police Chief tells Tod that Janie has tried to commit suicide shortly before. However, Linc feels that Janie's parents are themselves responsible for Jamie's condition. Then Janie's boyfriend Bill Caldwell and two friends attack Linc. After beating them in a brawl, Linc decides to leave town. Tod makes him see that he can't leave the girl in her depressed state. Linc rushes to find Janie. He finds her on a pleasure pier. She jumps overboard. Linc rescues her and finally makes her realize that happiness is within her grasp if she learns to face reality.

Cast: Tod (*Martin Milner*), Linc (*Glenn Corbett*), Janie (*Anne Helm*), Mr. Nickerson (*Alan Hale*), Mrs. Nickerson (*Phyllis Hill*), Paul (*Pat Renella*), Chief of Police (*Warren Kemmerling*), Bill Caldwell (*James O'Hara*).

#87. The Cruelest Sea of All

Executive Producer: **Herbert B. Leonard**
Written by: **Stirling Silliphant**
Directed by: **James Sheldon**

In Florida, Tod goes to work as Underwater Maintenance Man at an underwater theatre featuring the aquatic skill of thirty girl swimmers. The audience sits behind a circle of windows separating them from the underwater pool. Meanwhile, Lincoln Case gets a job at the Indian Village. After a performance of the swimmers, Elissa swims into the pool. Tod can't believe the length of time she is able to stay underwater. Tod meets Elissa in the room above the pool. Impressed by her aquatic skills, although baffled by her strange, halting speech, Tod tells her to apply for a job. He finds himself drawn to her.

Later, after being hired, Elissa meets Tod and Linc at a bar. Their efforts to learn her identity and origin prove fruitless as she gives them the name of a strange, unrecognizable place. She tells Tod she has come from her distant home because she has heard that people love each other for love, not because it is the season for love. She tells Tod she loves him. Later, she overreacts when she sees Tod paying attention to another girl.

Tod tells Linc that Elissa may be a phony. However, he can't resist the attraction she has for him. Finally Elissa realizes that Tod doesn't believe her. When Elissa asks Tod to return to the sea with her to prove his love, she sees the horror-stricken look in his eyes. She dives into the Gulf and disappears.

Cast: Tod (*Martin Milner*), Linc (*Glenn Corbett*), Elissa (*Diane Baker*), Donald McTaggart (*Edward Binns*), Anne Bradley (*Paula Stewart*), Paul Stace (*Jack Stamberger*), Woman Clerk (*Peggy Workinger*).

#88. Peace, Pity, Pardon

Executive Producer: **Herbert B. Leonard**
Written by: **Stirling Silliphant**
Directed by: **Robert Ellis Miller**

In Tampa, Tod and Linc find lodging at a home where ten jai alai players are boarding. Two of the players, Quiepo and Ramos Valera, are brothers who bitterly oppose the activities of their brother, one of Castro's chief aides. Largo is responsible for the death of many of their friends in Cuba. Quiepo, a patriot, has been instrumental in smuggling many people from Cuba. Both brothers know he is being watched. At first, Quiepo feels Tod and Linc are spying on him. When he learns the truth, he and his brother become friendly with Tod and Linc. Quiepo receives a message from Largo to meet him in a set rendezvous. Ramos warns Quiepo that it is a trap. Lacking knowledge of boats, Quiepo asks Tod and Linc to help him. Although Tod refuses to go, Linc gives his assent. When the speedboat is ready to leave, Tod is there.

At the rendezvous, they are met by a Cuban patrol boat. Quiepo goes aboard. Largo has his young daughter, Carlotta with him. He tells Quiepo he wants him to take her to the States for safekeeping. The Captain of the patrol boat appears with a submachine gun. He tells Largo it is his duty to capture Quiepo. In the fight that follows, Largo, Quiepo and the Captain are killed. Linc gets Carlotta to Tod and they speed away. The patrol boat catches up with them. Linc tosses a Molotov cocktail into the patrol boat, blowing it up. Linc and Tod bring Carlotta back to Ramos, the last of the embattled brothers.

Cast: Tod (*Martin Milner*), Linc (*Glenn Corbett*), Quiepo, (*Alejandro Rey*), Largo (*Michael Tolan*), Ramos (*Victor Gabriel*), Mrs. Foglesong (*Bibi Osterwald*), Teacher (*Coco Ramirez*), Carlotta (*Linda Bruhl*), Boat Captain (*Jose Duval*), Julio (*Charles Gonzales*).

#89. What a Shining Young Man Was Our Gallant Lieutenant

Executive Producer: **Herbert B. Leonard**
Written by: **Howard Rodman**
Directed by: **James Goldstone**

In Florida, Linc persuades Tod to visit Lieutenant School under whom he served in Vietnam. Linc doesn't know that "Lieutenant" was badly wounded in battle. He lives with his parents and two brothers, Paul and Thaddeus. Now in his early thirties, "Lieutenant" has forgotten everything that happened before his brain injury and has the mind of an eight-year-old child. Linc, over Tod's protests, decides he must spend some time with him. Twelve-year-old Beth Pritchard, daughter of a nearby farmer, is a friend of "Lieutenant." "Lieutenant" shows Linc an old car concealed beneath a hay tarpaulin. It was abandoned long before. "Lieutenant" has restored it; even the motor runs. However, it has no wheels and is supported by boxes under the axles.

More and more, Linc is drawn into "Lieutenant's" world. Linc buys four wheels for the car. He tells "Lieutenant" that he is going to take him for a long drive. "Lieutenant" feels in his mind that the car which he plans to give his mother for a birthday present is being taken from him. Finally, Linc comes to his senses, realizing he can't help "Lieutenant." On his mother's birthday, "Lieutenant" shows his mother the car. He is happy when she gets into the front seat beside him, his father and brothers in the back seat, and the car, motor running, propped up on boxes, is off in "Lieutenant's" mind to a far city. Tod and Linc drive away.

Cast: Tod (*Martin Milner*), Linc (*Glenn Corbett*), Lieutenant School (*Dick York*), Mrs. School (*Jane Rose*), Paul School (*James Brown*), Mr. School (*John Litel*), Thad School (*James Olson*), Beth (*Dianna Ramey*), Dock Foreman (*Arnold Soboloff*), Barmaid (*Carole Ann Lewis*).

#90. But What Do You Do in March?

Executive Producer: **Herbert B. Leonard**
Written by: **Stirling Silliphant**
Directed by: **Robert Ellis Miller**

Sidney Brooks and Midge Pierrepont, two beautiful and wealthy heiresses, have been rivals since childhood. While Midge has stuck to sports, Sidney has added fortune upon fortune to the original one left by her father. Tod and Linc became entrapped in the girls' rivalry when Midge's speedboat upsets the boat in which they are fishing. They go ashore to even matters and learn that Sidney has had a boat built to challenge Midge's preeminence in the big race sponsored by Guy Lombardo. Sidney refuses Midge's offer to drop their long-time rivalry. She vows to beat Midge. Sidney, using her beauty and money, gets Linc to sign a contract to drive her boat.

Tod warns Linc that Sidney will throw him aside after she has used him. Tod asks Sidney not to use Linc. When she refuses, he offers to drive Midge's boat. Sidney plays Linc along and he falls for her completely. When Linc tells him that he is leaving with Sidney after the race, Tod vows to beat him. Bix, Midge's chief mechanic, goes over the boat with Tod before the race. Linc, driving Sidney's boat, wins and he prepares to leave with her. After Sidney offers to pay him off, Linc knows that despite her promises, he is through. Tod and Linc realize that there is more to racing than speed as Midge races off in her boat while, high above, Sidney zooms away in her plane.

Cast: Tod (*Martin Milner*), Linc (*Glenn Corbett*), Sidney Brooks (*Janice Rule*), Midge Pierrepont (*Susan Kohner*), Woman (*Kay Medford*), Husband (*Paul Reed*), Bix (*Sammy Shore*).

#91. Who Will Cheer My Bonny Bride?"

Executive Producer: **Herbert B. Leonard**
Written by: **Shimon Wincelberg**
Directed by: **James Goldstone**

After their car runs out of gas on a country road in Florida, Tod and Linc split up to get help. Linc accepts a lift from Alvah Clayborne and his cousin, Charley, a sadistic psychotic. Charley has convinced Alvah that Lucy Joy is madly in love with him and is waiting to marry him in their hometown of Eubanks. Only her father stands between them. Charley has also convinced Alvah that they must show up for the wedding on the following morning with plenty of spending money. As a result, they hold up the Crystal Springs Motel, while Linc is outside. In the shooting that follows, Alvah is hit. With a gun at his head, Linc is forced to drive the two away. Although Charley, trigger-happy, wants to shoot Linc, Linc convinces him that only his efforts can keep Alvah alive. Later Tod gets to the motel and learns that Linc is suspected of complicity in the holdup.

Meanwhile, in his struggle to survive, Linc not only is forced to hold up a motorist, but manages to get through a roadblock. News is carried by the motorist whom Linc held up that Alvah and Charley are on their way to Eubanks. A posse is deputized to meet them. However, Alvah, Linc and Charley get to the church. When Alvah sees the bridegroom with his happy bride, he realizes that Charley has lied to him. The trio leave the church and shooting breaks out. Charley is killed. Alvah is bewildered until Linc makes him realize that Charley hated him and used him for a patsy all his life. After wishing Lucy Joy happiness, Alvah gives himself up to the police. Linc rejoins Tod.

#91. Who Will Cheer My Bonny Bride? (Cont'd)

Cast: Tod (*Martin Milner*), Linc (*Glenn Corbett*), Alvah Clayborne (*Rip Torn*), Charley (*Albert Salmi*), Sheriff Lemoine (*C. M. Gampel*), Motorist (*Gene Hackman*), Motel Cashier (*Marilynn Lovell*), Mr. Ginley (*George Mathews*), Deputy Keefer (*Dick Thies*), Bellhop (*Dan Morgan*), Lucy Joy (*Carol Shands*), Motel Manager (*Chuck Ross*), Eubanks Sheriff (*Joe Young*).

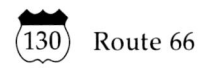

#92. Shadows of an Afternoon

Executive Producer: **Herbert B. Leonard**
Written by: **Leonard Freeman and Eric Scott**
Directed by: **James Sheldon**

Tod and Linc are able to rent a house cheaply in Florida by agreeing to care for the owner's dog and garden. As Linc finishes bandaging the dog whose belly had been badly ripped, he is arrested by two deputy sheriffs. He learns that he has been accused by Mrs. Bowers, a neighbor, of stabbing the dog with a pair of pruning shears. He is taken to jail. Walt Miller, a newspaperman, learns of his heroic war record and plays the story up big. Tod and Judith Kane hear a radio report of Linc's arrest. Judith works for Parker Smith, a lawyer. Parker agrees to defend Linc. However, he feels that the aristocratic Mrs. Bowers' testimony will definitely result in Linc's conviction in the small town. Parker is frustrated when Linc refuses to use his enviable war record as a defense. However, Parker delves into Mrs. Bowers' past.

During the trial, Parker brings forward two six-year-old girls, Rachel Morrison and Carla Lord. They testify the dog was badly injured when he tried to jump a sharp fence. Under Parker's questioning, Mrs. Bowers admits her husband was not the hero she claimed he was, but a vicious brute. She adds that Linc bears an amazing resemblance to her husband, and when she saw him holding a pair of pruning shears, and the dog yelping with pain, she visualized what her husband would have done. Linc is acquitted. Before driving from town with Tod, he expresses regret to Mrs. Bowers for his unfortunate part in bringing up a horrible period in her life.

#92. Shadows of an Afternoon (Cont'd)

Cast: Tod (*Martin Milner*), Linc (*Glenn Corbett*), Mrs. Bowers (*Miriam Hopkins*), Parker Smith (*Ralph Meeker*), Judith Kane (*Kathryn Hays*), Deputy Sam Harris (*Michael Conrad*), Walt Miller (*Richard Hamilton*), Mrs. LeMay (*Nydia Westman*), Mrs. Malcomb (*Dorothy Sands*), Judge Benton (*Cliff Hall*), Mr. Bell (*Roy Fant*), Carl (*Philip Bruns*), County Prosecutor (*Richard Mulligan*), 2nd Deputy (*Clifford Pellow*), Rachel (*Diane Higgins*), Carla (*Valerie Trill*), Kimberly Jo (*Francie Meyers*).

#93. Soda Pop and Paper Flags

Executive Producer: **Herbert B. Leonard**
Written by: **John McGreevey**
Directed by: **Fred Jackman**

In Mapleton, Florida, Tod goes for hamburgers while Linc remains at the garage while the car is being repaired. Tod sees Tim Pierce, Mike Weiser and Johnny Simmons molesting Emmett McNeill, a hobo. He goes to Emmett's defense. George Simmons, Johnny's father, and Andy Ferguson, owner of a rubber processing plant, drive up and stop the fight. Simmons apologizes for the actions of his son. Ferguson offers Tod and Emmett jobs in his plant to prove the good will of the town. Linc, refusing to join Tod at the plant, goes to work as a salesman. Later, Don, George Simmons' younger son, and Peter Ferguson, fall ill with a rare type of sleeping sickness.

Jim Horst, buyer for a group of discount stores, proves to be Linc's first customer. When Horst, a married man, shows that his only interest is to have Linc join him in dating two girls, Linc leaves and loses his job. Meanwhile, after giving blood tests to Emmett and Tod, Dr. Glazer finds that Emmett has the bacilli in his blood.

Simmons gathers a mob to take care of Emmett. Emmett who has been running all his life refuses to leave town. Tod pleads with Ferguson to help avert a tragedy. Ferguson's statement that he will fight for Emmett disperses the mob. Dr. Glazer finds that a dog Ferguson had bought for his son's birthday brought the disease-carrying ticks to town. Linc rejoins Tod as Emmett leaves on a freight train.

Cast: Tod (*Martin Milner*), Linc (*Glenn Corbett*), Whit Spencer (*Joseph Campanella*), Emmett McNeill (*Chester Morris*), Jim Horst (*Tom Bosley*), George Simmons (*Clifton James*), Andy Ferguson (*Frank Overton*), Johnnie Simmons (*Marco St. John*), Doctor Glazer (*Alan Alda*), Pete Ferguson (*Thomas Norden*), Don Simmons (*John Bartley Messenger*), Truck Driver (*Bruce Glover*).

ROUTE 66 – FOURTH SEASON

Episode Title	Air Date
94. Two Strangers and an Old Enemy	9/27/63
95. Same Picture, Different Frame	10/4/63
96. Come Out, Come Out Wherever You Are	10/11/63
97. Where Are the Sounds of Celli Brahms?	10/18/63
98. Build Your Houses with Their Backs to the Sea	10/25/63
99. And Make Thunder His Tribute	11/1/63
100. The Stone Guest	11/8/63
101. I Wouldn't Start from Here	11/15/63
102. A Cage In Search of a Bird	11/29/63
103. A Long Way from St. Louie	12/6/63
104. Come Home Greta Inger Gruenschaffen	12/13/63
105. 93 Percent in Smiling	12/20/63
106. Child of a Night	1/3/64
107. Is It True There are Poxies at the Bottom of Landfair Lake?	1/10/64
108. Like This It Means Father, Like This Bitter, Like This Tiger	1/17/64
109. Kiss the Monster, Make Him Sleep	1/24/64
110. Cries of Persons Close to One	1/31/64
111. Who in His Right Mind Needs a Nice Girl?	2/7/64
112. This is Going to Hurt Me More Than it Hurts You	2/14/64
113. Follow the White Dove with the Broken Wing	2/21/64
114. Where There's a Will, There's a Way (1)	3/6/64
115. Where There's a Will, There's a Way (2)	3/13/64

#94. Two Strangers and an Old Enemy

Executive Producer: **Herbert B. Leonard**
Written by: **Stirling Silliphant**
Directed by: **Walter Grauman**

In the Florida Everglades, Tod and Linc meet Major Barben, a WW II Veteran, and Takasuka, a former Japanese officer who are still fighting the war.

Cast: Tod (*Martin Milner*), Linc (*Glenn Corbett*), Takasuka (*Sessue Hayakawa*), Barben (*Jack Warden*), Vi Barben (*Nancy Wickwire*), Royce (*James Brown*), Reporter (*Dan Frazer*), Reporter on Deck (*Anthony Zerbe*).

#95. Same Picture, Different Frame

Executive Producer: **Herbert B. Leonard**
Written by: **Stirling Silliphant**
Directed by: **Philip Leacock**

Tod and Linc are working at Poland Spring, a summer resort in Maine. Tod is being pursued by Binky, the teenage daughter of Dr. Klein, an analyst, who feels her actions are normal for a girl of her age. After many years absence, Mrs. Morgan Harper returns to her home in Poland Spring. Morgan finds that her first husband, Eric, having escaped from an asylum, has followed her. Although the sheriff has Morgan guarded constantly, Linc saves Morgan's life after a blast from Eric's shotgun kills one man. Answering her need for protection, Linc learns that Eric, a psychotic artist, forced Morgan to pose with male models. Incited by the duplicity he himself had instigated, Eric set fire to his studio. Morgan, fleeing his homicidal rage, escaped through the studio skylight. Pursuing her, Eric was hit by falling glass, and lost the sight of one eye.

As Morgan finishes telling Linc her story, Eric, who has been trailing them, appears armed with a shotgun. He forces them to drive to the Mansion House, where he has killed a guard. Meanwhile, Dr. Klein and his wife, realizing they have been wrong in their treatment of Binky, free Tod of her unwelcome attentions by taking her home. At the Mansion House, Eric, shotgun in one hand, forces Linc and Morgan to pose for him. Linc throws Eric off guard, and Morgan escapes from the house. Eric pursues her and is fatally shot by deputies alerted by Tod.

Cast: Tod (*Martin Milner*), Linc (*Glenn Corbett*), Morgan (*Joan Crawford*), Eric (*Patrick O'Neal*) Dr. Sumner Klein (*Tom Bosley*), Binky (*Jacqueline Courtney*).

#96. Come Out, Come Out, Wherever You Are

Executive Producer: **Herbert B. Leonard**
Written by: **Richard Jessup, Anthony Basta and Stirling Silliphant**
Directed by: **Alvin Ganzer**

Tod and Linc, working in a sawmill on coastal Maine, room with Poppa Duplessis and his daughter Marie. She tells Tod she knows she must hurt Linc, who has fallen in love with her. At a bar, Tod and Linc rush to the aid of Jack Martinson who has started a fight on discovering he has been cheated at cards. Jack receives a bad scalp wound. Jack insists on returning with Tod and Linc to the Duplessis home where a birthday party for Marie has started. Marie treats Jack's wound. Although Linc has told him that Marie is his girl, Jack makes a play for her to which Marie immediately responds. Linc and Jack fight over Marie. Tod spanks Marie for her behavior. Marie steals the keys to the Corvette and drives off with Jack.

After hours spent in an amusement park, Jack tells Marie that despite her reaction to his lovemaking, she doesn't care for anybody; and in the same manner in which he sails from port to port, she drifts from man to man. Marie realizes she must find herself. When Jack returns to the Duplessis home alone, Linc starts a fight; Jack offers no defense. He tells Linc he is going back to sea. Later, Marie returns, determined to leave home to find herself. However, Linc makes the awakening girl realize that the only place she can truly find herself is at home.

Cast: Tod (*Martin Milner*), Linc (*Glenn Corbett*), Marie (*Diane Baker*), Poppa (*Lon Chaney, Jr.*), Jack (*Alex Cord*), Fortune Teller (*Louise Larabee*), Bartender (*Albert Henderson*), Card Dealer (*Peter Gumeny*).

#97. Where are the Sounds of Celli Brahms?

Executive Director: **Herbert B. Leonard**
Written by: **Stirling Silliphant**
Directed by: **Allen Miner**

Because he is the millionth driver to cross downtown Minneapolis during the Aquatennial, Linc is told by Shagbag, a publicity man, that he is to be a judge in the Miss Downtown Minneapolis Beauty Contest. At the Sheraton Ritz, Tod is assigned to work with Celli Brahms, a brilliant acoustical engineer, who is doing a decibel count of the hotel. Using self-hypnosis, Celli has beefed herself up to finish the job in seventy-two hours. Mr. Fenton, top hotel chain executive, is secretly following her work to judge whether she would make a good vice-president.

While Tod is falling asleep on his feet trying to keep up with Celli, Linc meets and falls for Valerie Mills, a girl from a humble background. Linc, having turned down invitations from other contestants because of Valerie, learns that she has entered the beauty contest. Tod feels his romantic efforts have failed to get through to Celli's career-imprisoned personality. However, Celli begins wondering whether she is paying too high a price for a vice-presidency.

Linc, after deciding what winning the contest might do to Valerie's life, finally votes for her, and she wins. Shortly before Tod collapses, Celli finally breaks out, banging cymbals, creating a noisy confusion wherever she goes. Celli and Tod are arrested. After bailing Tod out, Fenton sees Celli sleeping in her cell, and lets it be known that when she wakes up, she will be a vice-president.

Cast: Tod (*Martin Milner*), Linc (*Glenn Corbett*), Celli Brahms (*Tammy Grimes*), Fenton (*Horace McMahon*), Shagbag (*Harry Bellaver*), Valerie Mills (*Kelly Peters*), Mr. Savel (*William Post, Jr.*), Bartender (*Joseph Leon*).

#98. Build Your Houses with Their Backs to the Sea

Executive Producer: **Herbert B. Leonard**
Written by: **Frank R. Pierson**
Directed by: **Frank R. Pierson**

On the Maine Coast, Linc is working for Thayer Faxon, a lobster man, while Tod works for Ella Fulcher who runs clambakes for tourists. Menemsha Faxon, Faxon's son and Ella's husband, returns home after a long absence. Learning that his brother Robbie has drowned at sea, Menemsha goes berserk. Knowing that his brother feared the sea, Menemsha holds his father responsible for his death. Thayer tells Linc that lobstermen are stealing each others' traps. Although Ella is troubled by Menemsha's irresponsibility and his hatred for his father, she loves him. Another fight erupts when Menemsha accuses his family of not accepting his wife.

Menemsha, learning a son was born during his absence, tries to make a go of life with Ella, but finds his hatred of his father is too great. Menemsha cuts his father's traps. Thayer Faxon has stated that all thieves must be treated alike. Faxon tells Ella to bring her son to the Faxon home. Then he goes to sea with his son. Their empty dory is found, proof that father and son have resolved their differences in death. After delivering Ella and her baby to Abigail, Faxon's wife, Linc and Tod drive off.

Cast: Tod (*Martin Milner*), Linc (*Glenn Corbett*), Thayer Faxon (*Pat Hingle*), Menemsha (*William Shatner*), Abigail Faxon (*Audra Lindley*), Hollis (*Robert Dryden*), Ella (*Louise Sorel*), Mayhew (*Griff Evans*), Rolly (*Don McHenry*), David (*Bill Jessome*), Samuel (*Lloyd R. Knight*), Constable (*Thomas J. McCormack*).

#99. And Make Thunder His Tribute

Executive Producer: **Herbert B. Leonard**
Written by: **Lewis John Carlino**
Directed by: **Leonard Horn**

In Minnesota, Tod and Linc get jobs on Mike Donato's raspberry farm. There are two other workers, Vinny Culpepper, and Joe Sky, a Chippewa. Mike, sixty-five, constantly battles with his son Tony about methods of running the farm. A difference of opinion about how to scare birds away from the crops leads to a fight between father and son. Jenny, Tony's wife, stops the fight. Tony, his wife, and their infant son leave the farm. Tod expresses his admiration of Mike's strong will, but Linc, remembering his own past, feels the situation is ugly and stupid.

Mike's initial fumbling effort to bring Tony back fails. Mike sets up a meeting with Mr. Hawthorne, a banker, and Mr. Whitney, an architect, to build a motel on the farm, which Tony has always wanted to do. The meeting which Tony attends, ends up in a brawl when Mike's desire to keep a half-acre for planting completely upsets the architectural plans.

A heavy rainfall threatens the crops. Mike leads Linc, Tod and Joe in Herculean efforts to save the plants. Tony arrives just as his father is stricken with a heart attack. As Mike lies dying, the man who fought for everything in life explains to Tony that he has always meant the farm to be his. Telling Tony to build the motel, Mike asserts he has really won his battle since he feels he has a son who loves him—a son just like himself. Tod and Linc drive away.

Cast: Tod (*Martin Milner*), Linc (*Glenn Corbett*), Mike Donato (*J. Carrol Naish*), Joe Sky (*Alfred Ryder*), Tony (*Lou Antonio*), Vinny (*Michael J. Pollard*), Jenny (*Linda Marsh*), Mr. Whitney (*Thomas A. Carlin*).

#100. The Stone Guest

Executive Producer: **Herbert B. Leonard**
Written by: **Stirling Silliphant**
Directed by: **Allen Miner**

"Don Giovanni," the story of a libertine finally dragged down to hell for his sins, is the opening opera at the Annual Central City, Colorado Festival. Tod is working at the Opera House while Linc works for Ben Belden. Ben owns an old gold mine whose safety has been questioned. Ben was in the army with Linc. He is married and has three children. His wife Nora is about to give birth to a fourth. Feeling trapped by his family, and driven by a gnawing desire to find a place in life, Ben has become a brawler and a libertine.

While Linc and Tod search for him, Ben enters a saloon where Hazel Quine, a woman in her forties, who feels life has passed her by, is sitting with her brother Jimmy and his bride, Sue. After a brief clash, Ben leaves. Hazel follows him. Ben takes Hazel to his mine. The mine caves in, blocking their escape. Meanwhile, Nora's baby is born. News is received of the cave-in, and Charley Praeger, aided by Linc and Tod, starts rescue operations. With their air supply running out, and certain that no one knows they are in the mine, Ben tells Hazel he plans to blast an exit with a large amount of dynamite.

On the surface, Tod cautions David, Ben's son, who senses the relationship between Don Giovanni and Ben, not to judge his father. With Hazel's hands over his, Ben sets off the blast. There is a thundering crash, and then, for Ben and Hazel—nothing.

Cast: Tod (*Martin Milner*), Linc (*Glenn Corbett*), Hazel Quine (*Jo Van Fleet*), Ben Belden (*Lee Philips*), Nora Belden (*Marion Ross*), David Belden (*Christopher Votos*), Jimmy Quine (*William Cort*), Sue Quine (*Brooke Bundy*), Doctor (*Harold Gould*), Sheriff (*Oliver McGowan*), Charley Praeger (*Crahan Denton*).

#101. I Wouldn't Start From Here

Executive Producer: **Herbert B. Leonard**
Written by: **Ernest Kinoy**
Directed by: **Allen Miner**

During a heavy rainstorm in Vermont, Tod and Linc are forced to spend the night at the farm of Arthur Perham, a widower in his late sixties. Perham is close to defeat in his lifelong battle to eke out a living from the rock-laden earth. He is forced to admit he cannot withstand another winter alone. He agrees to auction off his home to get sufficient funds to pay his debts and enter a home for the aged. After seeing Claire, the attractive daughter of a summer resident, Tod and Linc accept Perham's offer to work for him for two weeks. Tod is drawn to Claire, who is aware of the distinction between the summer visitor and the year-long resident who must struggle to survive.

Perham is present at the auction of his farm and possessions. His team of horses is put up for sale. Perham prizes the horses. The previous year he and his team came in second in a weight-drawing contest. With Linc doing the bidding, Perham buys the horses himself. Perham enters the team in one last contest. He coaches Tod and Linc to assist him. Arthur loses because of Tod's and Linc's inexperience. Linc offers to help him through the winter. Perham tells him he is selling the team. Tod and Linc stand silently as Perham walks off behind his horses to meet the fate he has staved off all his life.

Cast: Tod (*Martin Milner*), Linc (*Glenn Corbett*), Arthur Perham (*Parker Fennelly*), Claire (*Rosemary Forsyth*), Frank Ball (*Howard Freeman*), Newton Wheeler (*John Gibson*).

#102. A Cage in Search of a Bird

Executive Producer: **Herbert B. Leonard**
Written by: **Stirling Silliphant**
Directed by: **James Sheldon**

In Denver, Julie Severn, a confederate of card sharp Rick Mango, is trapped by a cheated player. She draws a gun, takes $600 from the table, and escapes. Badly beaten by the players, Rick follows her. Frantic, Julie eludes him by driving off with Tod and Linc. Later she hides the money in a hub cap of the Corvette. Rick arrives with two policemen, and claims Julie has robbed him. Len Ringsby, a stranger, saves Julie by claiming she is his niece. Julie is forced to remain with Len. Hoping to retrieve the money, Julie arranges to meet Linc in Denver.

Len is the surviving member of a gang which staged a $250,000 holdup of the U.S. Mint in Denver thirty-three years before. All he has left is a scrapbook about the holdup. Len believes that by helping Julie, he can find meaning in life. He tells her that she can collect a $25,000 reward by turning him in to the police.

Although Rick manages to get the $600, Tod saves Julie from Rick's savagery. Then Julie discovers she has lost Len's scrapbook. Rick, who has found the scrapbook and turned Len in, bitterly tells Julie there was no reward. Visiting Len in jail, Julie tells him she turned him in as he had requested, and is using the money to finance her future. Outside, Julie, who lied about the non-existent reward, bids farewell to Tod and Linc.

Cast: Tod (*Martin Milner*), Linc (*Glenn Corbett*), Jay Leonard Ringsby (*Dan Duryea*), Julie (*Stefanie Powers*), Rick (*Alex Cord*), Police Officer (*Bert Remsen*), Mr. Blees (*Donald J. Finnie*), Waitress (*Betty Mumey*).

Fourth Season

#103. A Long Way from St. Louie

Executive Producer: **Herbert B. Leonard**
Written by: **Stirling Silliphant**
Directed by: **Alvin Ganzer**

Sightseeing in a helicopter piloted by Lawrence Foxglove, Tod and Linc see five girls sleeping in the empty stadium of the Toronto Exposition Park. The helicopter zooms down and Linc jumps onto the field. He learns that Liz Marshall, "Chops" McGuire, Daphne Moore, Allison Parnell, and Gyo Hatabishi, are a stranded musical quintet who have been evicted from their hotel. Linc brings the girls to the hotel room he shares with Tod. Tod refuses to join him in advancing the girls' fare back home. The girls leave. Meanwhile, Mrs. Longworth, credit manager of the girls' hotel, tells Linc she will return the girls' instruments if he can get them a booking. He is unable to do so. At a striptease joint, he gets into a brawl, and he and the girls are thrown in jail.

Tod bails them out and admits he is attracted to Liz. Tod and Linc give up their hotel room to the girls. Foxglove and four other young men arrive and start a party. Tod discovers the party. He forces them to leave. Later, anxious to make amends, Tod joins Linc in an unsuccessful search for the girls. The girls see a poster announcing their appearance at a benefit performance and credit Tod and Linc. However, Tod and Linc learn that Foxglove is responsible. He tells them he doesn't want this gallant act of his known because it would destroy his reputation as a cad.

Cast: Tod (*Martin Milner*), Linc (*Glenn Corbett*), Liz (*Jessica Walter*), Gyo (*Virginia Wing*), Allison (*Lynda Day*), Daphne (*Susan Ringwood*), Chops (*Patricia Harty*), Walt (*Al Lewis*), Foxglove (*Hedley Mattingly*).

#104. Come Home, Greta Inger Gruenschaffen

Executive Producer: **Herbert B. Leonard**
Written by: **Joel Carpenter**
Directed by: **Philip Leacock**

Led by Heiss Horgal, the Buffalo chapter of a group devoted to their belief in the vital relationship between brain and muscle, gather to bid farewell to Greta Inger Gruenschaffen. Greta is leaving on a mission to spread the good word. Unable to get Heiss to realize she is in love with him, Greta runs away. She arrives in a helicopter in Vermont, where Tod and Linc are working at a ski lodge. Tod and Linc immediately start vying for her attention. Heiss and his group make every effort to find Greta. Tod is deflated when Greta terms his knowledge of her cause superficial. Then Greta beats Linc in a series of physical contests, ranging from mountain climbing to swimming. Greta is drawn to Tod but he realizes her mind is elsewhere. Greta phones Heiss's home. However, realizing he is blind to her feeling for him, she hangs up without letting him know where she is.

Heiss, determined to find Greta for the sake of the cause, finally gets to the inn in Vermont. Greta hides in a cross beam above the main room of the lodge. When Linc and Tod try to stop Heiss from reaching her, he outfights both of them. Listening to Greta, Linc and Tod realize she loves Heiss. Linc finally gets this through to Heiss. As Greta is leaving in a helicopter, Heiss shouts his love to her. She returns. Tod and Linc watch them fly off together.

Cast: Tod (*Martin Milner*), Linc (*Glenn Corbett*), Greta (*Tammy Grimes*), Heiss Horgal (*Chad Everett*), Mr. Spofford (*William LeMassena*).

#105. 93 Percent in Smiling

Executive Producer: **Herbert B. Leonard**
Producer: **Leo Davis**
Written by: **Alvin Sargent**
Directed by: **Philip Leacock**

On the Erie Canal Tod and Linc stop a fight between Aaron Kronberg, a fellow worker, and Haskell, their boss. Haskell fires Aaron. Aaron, his wife Min, and their children, Howard 11, Pansy 9, and Rudy 8 months old, live in a trailer near Tod and Linc's. Aaron has lost job after job because he feels his work is beneath him. Pansy is determined to save Rudy from their gypsy-like existence. After searching for a family with a normal way of life, Pansy and Howard decide the Macklins would give Rudy a decent upbringing. Before dawn, Pansy and Howard leave their trailer with Rudy. Linc sees them but is unaware of their purpose. Pansy and Howard find the Macklins have moved. They leave Rudy with Billy Hinkley, a boy of Howard's age, overnight. The next day, after policemen start investigating the kidnapping, the children take Rudy to the empty Macklin house.

Later, Linc, puzzled by the children's actions when he saw them before dawn, trails them to the Macklin house. Although Linc and Tod fail to get Aaron to see his children are disturbed by their rootless existence, they take him to the empty house. The crushing truth finally reaches Aaron when he overhears Pansy, who wishes to go further to ensure Rudy's happiness, give in to Howard's demand that they return with Rudy to the trailer. Aaron quietly leaves, followed by Tod and Linc. When Pansy and Howard bring Rudy to the trailer, they realize from their father's reception that life will be brighter for all in the future.

Cast: Tod (*Martin Milner*), Linc (*Glenn Corbett*), Aaron Kronberg (*Albert Salmi*), Howard (*David Howell*), Pansy (*Susan Howell*), Min Kronberg (*Olga Bellin*), Mrs. Snyder (*Jean Stapleton*).

#106. Child of a Night

Executive Producer: **Herbert B. Leonard**
Written by: **Stirling Silliphant**
Directed by: **Allen Miner**

Before dying, Gerald Ward, the lone survivor of a plane crash, asks Linc to find the child of Lonnie, a waitress he had met in a Savannah tavern over twenty years before. He turns over thirty-eight thousand dollars for Linc to give to this unknown child of his brief love affair. Linc hires an attorney named Warren, runs ads and checks the Registrar of Vital Statistics. Linc and Tod also search for the tavern in which Lonnie worked. They follow many false leads, including one presented by Millie Wilkens, and another by Marty Johnson, a young man abandoned at the same time Lonnie had her child. Harry, who is the present owner of the tavern where Lonnie worked, tells Tod and Linc that Lonnie is in Madison House, the local poor-house. Lonnie doesn't tell them to whom she gave the baby.

Mrs. Barber, a midwife, sends them to Mr. Hull, a school janitor, who once owned the tavern where Lonnie worked. Hull tells them he and his deceased wife brought up Nita, Lonnie's daughter, to believe she was their child. He feels the truth would destroy Nita's life. Tod and Linc find that Nita, owner of a small decorating establishment, is living in a dream world imagining that each of her successive wealthy young clients will marry her. Hull finally tells Nita the truth. The shock is agonizing. However, before leaving Savannah, Linc and Ted drive Nita to Madison House for a reunion with Lonnie.

Cast: Tod (*Martin Milner*), Linc (*Glenn Corbett*), Lonnie Taylor (*Sylvia Sidney*), Mr. Hull (*Chester Morris*), Gerald Ward (*Herschell Bernardi*), Harry (*Percy Rodriguez*), Nita (*Diana Van der Vlis*).

#107. Is It True There are Poxies at the Bottom of Landfair Lake?

Executive Producer: **Herbert B. Leonard**
Producer: **Leo Davis**
Written by: **Alvin Sargent**
Directed by: **John Peyser**

Employed by a Savannah sign company, Tod and Linc drive in the company truck to Clawson to put up a neon sign over Judson Denker's general store. Simon Devereaux lassoes the sign and hauls it away. After fighting with Simon, Linc retrieves the damaged sign. All the townspeople, including Denker, are sympathetic to Simon who recently returned from Army duty. Simon is having bitter disputes with his father, Amos, an alcoholic, and is trying to keep his sister, Olivia, from taking a job in Savannah, by making her realize her only safety lies in a small town. Simon even rages against young Mel Harper, his friend, age nine. As the result of a phone call from Simon, Diana comes to town. In front of Tod and Linc and the men of the town, Simon tells how he was the butt of every prank the city boys in the Army could pull on him.

Simon relates how they had introduced him to Diana, and how he had fallen in love with her. In the presence of his city friends, he had gone through a marriage ceremony with her. Only after it was over, did he realize what her profession was. Everyone feels the humiliation Diana is suffering. Linc starts a fight with Simon. Amos, pulling them apart, slaps his son's face in disgust. Later, Tod goes to see Simon but leaves, feeling his attempts to change Simon's attitude have failed. Linc and Tod finish putting up the sign. Simon drives into town on his tractor. He asks Linc to allow his sister Olivia to drive with them in the truck on their way to Savannah.

Cast: Tod (*Martin Milner*), Linc (*Glenn Corbett*), Simon Devereaux (*Geoffrey Horne*), Amos Devereaux (*Crahan Denton*), Diana (*Collin Wilcox*).

#108. Like This it Means Father, Like This Bitter, Like this Tiger

Executive Producer: **Herbert B. Leonard**
Written by: **Stirling Silliphant**
Directed by: **Jeffrey Hayden**

Ted and Linc enter a Savannah tavern. Cam Wilcox is cadging drinks by giving imitations of theatrical personalities. Linc suddenly attacks him. Although Linc is arrested, Cam refuses to press charges. Linc tells Tod that Cam's cowardice during the war cost him the lives of two of his men. Linc adds that he has sworn to hound Cam until he admits his cowardice. Cam has a wife, Edith, and a son, Victor, age ten. Because of his alcoholism, he finds it difficult to get a job. Linc returns to the tavern. He forces Cam to imitate a soldier in action and makes him crawl. Vic enters and makes his father leave. Vic waits for Linc. He attacks Linc, after telling him he knows his father is a coward. Linc makes no effort to protect himself.

Linc waits for Vic at school. He tells Vic his father may be paying a higher price than the two men who died. Linc makes up with Cam. He takes him to the recreation room of an American Legion Hall. Together, Linc and Cam tell the story of the action they were involved in. Suddenly, the shame of Linc's trickery comes down on Cam. He tries to attack Linc with a bayonet, then forces him to accompany him home. Linc leaves after Cam tells Edith he has been living as a dead man because he refused to face the truth. Now, if she is willing to stay with him, he will stand up and face the world.

Cast: Tod (*Martin Milner*), Linc (*Glenn Corbett*), Cam Wilcox (*Larry Blyden*), Edith Wilcox (*Frances Helm*), Mr. King (*Eugene Roche*), Vic (*Donald Losby*), Bartender (*Clifford Fellow*), Eddie Winston (*Bill Lazarus*), Harry Comenzo (*James Dimitri*), Detective (*Leonard Hicks*), Men in Bar (*Joe Ponazecki, Ramon Bieri*).

Fourth Season

#109. Kiss the Monster—Make Him Sleep

Executive Producer: **Herbert B. Leonard**
Written by: **Stanley R. Greenberg**
Directed by: **Allen Reisner**

Nola Neilsen has long fought the domination of her brother, construction tycoon, Hamar Neilsen. Shortly after Tod and Linc go to work for Hamar Neilsen, Nola jumps from a bridge he is building across the Mississippi, in revenge for his latest act of interference. Linc rescues her and they become romantically involved. Linc becomes obsessed with the idea of rescuing Nola from her brother's domination. Linc's mother, Mrs. Case, comes to town. Feeling his father's influence warped his youth, Linc once again refuses to talk to him after his mother places a long distance call to her husband. When Linc asks Nola to join him and his mother, she asks him to go out with her alone. Leaving to join his mother, Linc tells Nola he will call her in the morning. Nola picks up Marks, a salesman.

Later Nola tells Hamar that Linc got her drunk and threw her out of her apartment. Hamar goes to see Linc. Despite Hamar's pleas that he give Nola up, Linc tells Hamar that he is determined to free Nola. Mrs. Case insinuates that Linc is going to fight his own father, not Hamar. Although her words almost penetrate, Linc follows Hamar. Linc is battering Hamar when Nola drives up with Marks. Linc finally understands that Hamar has been striving to save Nola from herself. Later Linc phones home and talks to his father for the first time in years.

Cast: Tod (*Martin Milner*), Linc (*Glenn Corbett*), Hamar Neilsen (*James Coburn*), Mrs. Case (*Linda Watkins*), Nola Neilsen (*Barbara Mattes*).

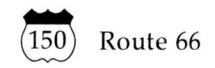

#110. Cries of Persons Close to One

Executive Producer: **Herbert B. Leonard**
Producer: **Leo Davis**
Written by: **William Kelley and Howard Rodman**
Directed by: **Allen Miner**

Tank, a third-rate fighter, brawls in an alcoholic state in and out of the ring. For years, Gaybee has traveled with him in a station wagon from one fight club to another, hoping some day Tank will change. At a drive-in where Tod and Linc have stopped for hamburgers, Tank gets the impression some of the local boys have been annoying Gaybee. He charges into them. One boy finally knocks Tank out with a football. Although Tod protests, Linc drives the station wagon to the next town where Tank is fighting for a much needed $165. Mr. Newton, the promoter, refuses Gaybee's request that Tank's bout be postponed.

Tank, warned by the doctor not to fight that night, awakens at a motel and begins drinking. Tod follows him to an empty school house. There the frustrations of a man unable to write his own name erupt. Tank imagines Tod to be the teacher who had failed him. He is about to fight Tod when he collapses. To get money for Gaybee and Tank, Linc substitutes for Tank at the bout. Tank awakens at the motel. Despite Gaybee's pleas, he insists on going to the ring. Linc is being beaten when Tank, flailing wildly, gets into the ring where he collapses.

Gaybee tells Tank she can't take any more and is leaving him. Linc excoriates Tank for his selfish disregard for Gaybee. Tank follows Gaybee. Gaybee throws herself into Tank's arms, when for the first time, he tells her that he loves her.

Cast: Tod (*Martin Milner*), Linc (*Glenn Corbett*), Tank (*Michael Parks*), Gaybee (*Ellen Madison*), Mr. Newton (*James Brown*), Blair (*Michael Baseleon*).

#111. Who in His Right Mind Needs a Nice Girl

Executive Producer: **Herbert B. Leonard**
Producer: **Leo Davis**
Written by: **Joel Carpenter**
Directed by: **Jeffrey Hayden**

Acting on Mr. Hendrickson's instructions, Joe Paris violently swerves a fishing cruiser. Mrs. Hendrickson falls overboard and drowns. Unaware that Joe has removed the bullets, Hendrickson shoots a revolver at Joe. Joe veers the boat until Hendrickson is flung overboard. Joe sinks the boat and swims to shore. In a library stockroom, Joe overpowers Lucy Brown, a librarian. Alternating between bursts of cruelty and appeals for help, Joe soon has Lucy completely spellbound. At the library, Linc realizes something is troubling Lucy. She denies it. Later, Linc and Tod return to the library. Joe enters and sits at a library table. Lucy finally tells Linc of her predicament. Joe agrees to leave with Tod and Linc. After clothing and feeding him, Tod and Linc drive Joe to the edge of town. Joe starts a fight with Tod and takes a beating.

Although Linc orders him to leave town, Joe returns to the library. Again Joe gets Lucy completely under his spell. After Lucy and Joe leave, Betty, another librarian, calls the police. Radio alarms are sent out for Joe. Tod and Linc meet Lucy as she leaves the bank with all her money for Joe. Realizing the truth of her statement that they have no right to interfere with her actions, Tod and Linc take her to Joe. She gives him the money. Joe turns down Lucy's offer to go away with him. Overtaken by a sheriff and his deputies, Joe refuses to surrender and runs away. Tod, Linc and Lucy watch as Joe is shot and killed.

Cast: Tod (*Martin Milner*), Linc (*Glenn Corbett*), Joe (*Lee Philips*), Lucy Brown (*Lois Smith*), Mrs. Harris (*Ruth McDevitt*), Mr. Richards (*Dan Frazer*), Betty (*Elizabeth MacRae*).

#112. This is Going to Hurt Me More Than It Hurts You

Executive Producer: **Herbert B. Leonard**
Written by: **Stirling Silliphant**
Directed by: **Alvin Ganzer**

In St. Augustine, Tod meets a former Yale classmate, Harlan Livingston III, a multi-millionaire, morbidly attracted only to beautiful girls who are ill. Aboard Harlan's yacht are Cindy, Andrea and Jeanelle, and Dr. Frank Hillman, Harlan's uncle. Hillman ministers to Harlan's sham invalids, each with an eye on Harlan's fortune. Dr. Hillman has promised to stay with Harlan for a year in exchange for a million dollar donation to his clinic. Harlan, fearful the three girls plan to sue him for breach of promise, offers Tod a thousand dollars to lure them off, but Tod refuses. Tod meets Doree Hunter, a beautiful, naive girl. Doree's mother, looking for a rich husband for her daughter, turns to Harlan, claiming Doree is suffering from a fatal illness.

Meanwhile, Harlan has hired Linc to pretend to be Tod's bodyguard and help give the impression that Tod is an eccentric millionaire. The three girls turn their attentions to Tod. Doree, however, who had a fondness for Tod, turns against him when she finds her mother playing up to him. Harlan, learning he needs a tonsillectomy, tells his uncle that the bequest for the clinic was his all along, but that he had inveigled him into a year's cruise because it was felt he was working too hard. Harlan and Doree discover their mutual need for each other. She holds his hand as he is wheeled into the operating room, while Tod and Linc wave goodbye.

Cast: Tod (*Martin Milner*), Linc (*Glenn Corbett*), Harlan Livingston, III (*Soupy Sales*), Doree Hunter (*Dawn Nickerson*), Mrs. Hunter (*Bibi Osterwald*), Dr. Frank Hillman (*Roland Winters*), Jeanelle (*Lee Meriwether*), Cindy (*Carole Ann Lewis*), Andrea (*Lorraine Rogers*).

#113. Follow the White Dove with the Broken Wing

Executive Producer: **Herbert B. Leonard**
Written by: **Alvin Sargent**
Directed by: **Denis Sanders**

In Florida, Tod and Linc run into Walter Reston who takes rejection seriously, at a coffeehouse hangout for teenagers. After Yvonne leaves Walter cold while they are dancing to take up with Warren Hughes, Arthur Santos, a policeman, tries to calm him down. Later Walter breaks away from Arthur and runs through a warehouse filled with crates. Walter playfully puts crates in Arthur's path. A pile of crates tumbles. Walter's arm is severely cut. Arthur is killed. Walter takes Arthur's gun and runs. Walter forces Tod and Linc to drive him to an unused building. Warren tells Police Captain West that the teenagers would like to help track Walter down. West tells them to keep out of it. Holding Linc as hostage, Walter sends Tod for medical supplies.

Mrs. Santos, Arthur's widow, becomes hysterical when Tod asks her to call off the teenagers' hunt before someone else is killed. After Captain West promises to do so to protect Linc's life, Tod tells him where Walter is. The teenagers, who have already confronted Walter's mother in their search, trail Tod. Although Tod pleads with them, the teenagers attack Walter. However, the pathetic sincerity of Walter's statement that he didn't mean to kill Santos touches them. Walter leaves. Grigsby, the prime mover of the attack, suddenly realizes he has no followers and he also leaves. Tod and Linc watch as Walter gives himself up to the police.

Cast: Tod (*Martin Milner*), Linc (*Glenn Corbett*), Walter Reston (*Lee Kinsolving*), Captain West (*Bert Freed*), Arthur Santos (*Victor Arnold*), Mrs. Santos (*Rose Gregorio*), Yvonne (*Jacqueline Courtney*), Grigsby (*Will Mackenzie*), Hilda (*Carole Demas*).

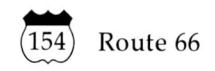

#114. Where There's a Will, There's a Way (Part I)

Executive Producer: **Herbert B. Leonard**
Written by: **Stirling Silliphant**
Directed by: **Alvin Ganzer**

The Tiffins, Otis, Michael, Leon and Samantha return to Tampa from the four corners of the earth to attend the funeral of their brother, Alexander. Alexander's will, read by his executor, Monty Musgrave, has been conceived with the idea of promoting mayhem between the members of the family. Each, including Alex's daughter Margo, is to receive one hundred thousand dollars on the condition that Margo marry his friend Tod Stiles, who is to receive an equal share, otherwise the fortune goes to Interpol. To carry out his macabre joke, Alexander has further stipulated that within two weeks after Margo's marriage, Monty is to give the remainder of the four million dollar estate to one of the family which, by that time, will include Tod. Linc tells Tod that he is going to South America to work in a native village.

Outraged at first by her part in her father's scheme, Margo changes after meeting Tod. Unaware that the Tiffins have forced Margo to meet him, Tod immediately falls in love with her. Margo tries to resist her attraction to Tod because she realizes the Tiffins, single or collectively, will try to kill him after their marriage. Immediately before the ceremony Tod learns his life is in jeopardy. After the wedding, Margo rushes Tod away to escape her murderous relatives. The driver tricks Tod out of a cab in the middle of a bridge. Before Margo's horrified eyes, the driver knocks Tod unconscious, flings him over the rail, and speeds away.

#114. Where There's a Will, There's a Way (Part I) (Cont'd)

Cast: Tod (*Martin Milner*), Linc (*Glenn Corbett*), Otis (*Roger C. Carmel*), Michael (*Alex Cord*), Samantha (*Nina Foch*), Leon (*Patrick O'Neal*), Monty Musgrave (*Chill Wills*), Margo (*Barbara Eden*), Russian Man (*Louis Zorich*), Lieutenant (*Victor Gabriel Junquera*), Thomboli (*Hugh Hurd*), European Man (*Rene Paul*), Driver (*Richard Kuss*).

#115. Where There's a Will, There's a Way (Part II)

Executive Producer: **Herbert A. Leonard**
Written by: **Stirling Silliphant**
Directed by: **Alvin Ganzer**

After his wedding to Margo Tiffin, Tod was tossed unconscious off a bridge. Otis, Michael, Leon and Samantha Tiffin begin maneuvering to get rid of another claimant. Linc joins the search for Tod, claiming Michael tricked him into going to South America. Tod escapes from a swamp and gets to Linc. Margo is overjoyed when she finds Tod is alive. Tod and Linc pose as wealthy German naturalists interested in swampland Leon has bought from Monty. Samantha, determined to get the residue of the estate, plays up to Monty.

Trying to sell the swampland to Tod and Linc, Leon disappears in the mud. Samantha marries Monty. Disguised as Latin American patriots, Tod and Linc convince Michael that their country is waiting for his return to become its leader. He flies there, unaware that Linc has exposed his machinations and that a firing squad waits to receive him. Tod and Linc find that two Russian agents are returning Otis to his adopted homeland because of the illegality of his money-making schemes.

Samantha is crushed when Monty decides not to give the remainder of the four million dollars to any of the survivors, but to give it to Interpol, the alternative expressed in the will. Linc tells Tod and Margo he is returning to Texas. Tod and Margo drive off on their deferred honeymoon.

Cast: Tod (*Martin Milner*), Linc (*Glenn Corbett*), Otis (*Roger C. Carmel*), Michael (*Alex Cord*), Samantha (*Nina Foch*), Leon (*Patrick O'Neal*), Monty Musgrave (*Chill Wills*), Margo (*Barbara Eden*), Russian Man (*Louis Zorich*), Lieutenant (*Victor Gabriel Junquera*), Thomboli (*Hugh Hurd*), European Man (*Rene Paul*), Driver (*Richard Kuss*).

#116. I'm Here to Kill a King*

Executive Producer: **Herbert B. Leonard**
Written by: **Stirling Silliphant**
Directed by: **Allen Reisner**

Tod and Linc are working at Niagara Falls. The King of an eastern country is scheduled to tour the area. Colonel Zaman, the King's aide, has hired Paul Cades to kill the King. Robin, Zaman's girlfriend, has been carrying on with Cades. Zaman and Robin are stunned by Tod's resemblance to Cades. Tod, who has received an envelope meant for Cades from Zaman, realizes something strange is happening. He goes to the Central Bureau of Intelligence before Cades catches up with him. Zaman orders Kahwaji to kill Cades after the King is assassinated. After shooting a government agent, Cades forces Tod to accompany him aboard a cabin cruiser. Pierson, an American official, tells the King of the relationship between Zaman and Cades.

The King forces Zaman to impersonate him at public affairs. Unable to bring himself to shoot Tod, Cades takes Linc as hostage to ensure Tod's silence. Linc thinks Cades is Tod. Still puzzled as Cades raises his rifle to shoot the King, Linc throws him off balance and runs from the hail of bullets. Cades shoots Zaman. As Cades raises his gun to shoot Tod who bars his escape, bullets from Kahwaji's Luger kill him. Tod and Linc, still unsure of what happened, stand together as agents swarm over the entire area.

Cast: Tod (*Martin Milner*), Linc (*Glenn Corbett*), Colonel Zaman (*Robert Loggia*), Robin (*Tina Louise*), King (*Arnold Moss*), Mr. Pierson (*Frank Campanella*), Kahwaji (*Jack Dabdoub*).

* <u>Author's Note</u>: "I'm Here To Kill a King" was originally scheduled to air on November 29, 1963 but was pre-empted due to the Kennedy assassination. Because of the similar subject matter, the episode was never shown on the network that season. It later aired in syndication. However, some sources claim, the episode was shown on March 20, 1964 a week after the final two-part episode "Where There's a Will, There's a Way."

ROUTE 66 PRODUCTION COMPANY

Executive Producer **Herbert B. Leonard**
Writer and Co-Creator **Stirling Silliphant**
Executive in Charge of Production **Sam Manners**
Producers:
   Leonard Freeman, Leo Davis, Mort Abrahms, and Robert Bassler
Associate Producers **Herb Stewart and Jerry Thomas**
Story Editor **Howard Rodman**
Director of Photography **Jack Marta and Irving Lippman**
Camera Operator **Robert Johannes**
Supervising Film Editor **Aaron Nibley**
Film Editor **Jack Gleason**
Second Unit Director **Leonard Katzman**
Assistant Directors **Max Stein and Bruce Bilson**
Original Music composed and conducted by **Nelson Riddle**
Orchestration **Gil Grau**
Music Supervisor **Edward Forsyth**
Art Director **John T. McCormack**
Set Decoration **William Calvert**
Script Supervisor **Jack Gannon**
Special Effects **Ira Anderson**
Costumes **Charles Arrico**
Makeup **Abe Haberman**
Property Master **Arthur Wasson**
Sound Mixer **Paul Franz**
Gaffer **Virgil Thompson**
Key Grip **Harold Sanders**
Sound Effects Editor **Jim Bullock**
Post Production Supervisor **Lawrence Werner**
Location Manager **John D. Benson**
Musician Contractor **Jack Lee**
Assistant to the Producer **Wiletta Leonard**

BIOGRAPHIES

Glenn Corbett

Glenn Corbett began his career as a contract player with Columbia Pictures in 1959. After a series of supporting and lead roles, he replaced George Maharis in *Route 66* in the spring of 1963. In the mid-60s, he co-starred in another TV series: *The Road West*. In addition to his many TV guest appearances, Corbett played supporting roles in several John Wayne westerns and in the war epic *Midway*. He later appeared as Paul Morgan in the long-running TV series *Dallas*.

His film credits include: *The Crimson Kimono, Man on a String, The Mountain Road, All the Young Men, Homicidal, Shenandoah, Chisum, Big Jake,* and *Midway*. TV appearances include: *It's a Man's World, Route 66, Twelve O'Clock High, The Virginian, The Legend of Jesse James, The Road West, Garrison's Gorillas, Star Trek, Land of the Giants, The Immortal, Marcus Welby, The FBI, Bonanza, Night Gallery, Medical Center, Alias Smith & Jones, Owen Marshall: Counselor at Law, The Mod Squad, Cannon, The Streets of San Francisco, Manhunter, Movin' On, Caribe, Police Woman, Petrocelli, Police Story, The Doctors, The Rockford Files, Barnaby Jones, Fantasy Island, The Fall Guy, Simon and Simon,* and *Dallas*.

Anne Francis

Beautiful as well as talented, Anne Francis began modeling as a child and by age 11 had graced the Broadway stage opposite Gertrude Lawrence in *Lady in the Dark*. She was later discovered by Daryl Zanuck and placed under contract to 20th Century Fox. Eventually, Anne signed with M.G.M. and co-starred in several classic films of the 1950s.

Anne Francis (Cont'd)

In the 1960s, she guest-starred in many network television series, and in 1965 she starred in the cult classic series *Honey West* for which she received an Emmy nomination, and won a Golden Globe Award.

For the past four decades, Anne has continued to appear in episodic TV, mini series and movies for television. She has also become an accomplished writer. She is the author of a book entitled "Voices from Home" and has written, produced and directed an art film, *Gemini Rising* that has aired on PBS.

Film credits include: *Summer Holiday, Elopement, Lydia Bailey, Dreamboat, A Lion in the Streets, The Rocket Man, Susan Slept Here, Rogue Cop, Bad Day at Black Rock, Battle Cry, Blackboard Jungle, The Scarlet Coat, Forbidden Planet, The Rack, The Hired Gun, Girl of the Night, The Crowded Sky, The Satan Bug, Brainstorm, The Love God, More Dead than Alive,* and *Funny Girl.*

Her many television credits include: *Studio One, Climax, Rawhide, Adventures in Paradise, The Untouchables, Hong Kong, Route 66, Dr. Kildare, The New Breed, Alcoa Premiere, The Twilight Zone, The Eleventh Hour, Arrest and Trial, Kraft Suspense Theatre, Temple Houston, Death Valley Days, The Reporter, Ben Casey, The Man from Uncle, The Alfred Hitchcock Hour, The Fugitive, The Invaders, Mission Impossible, The Name of the Game, Dan August, The Virginian, Love American Style, Insight, Archer, Movin' On, A Girl Named Sooner, Ellery Queen, Barnaby Jones, Petrocelli, S.W.A.T., Mobile One, Bert D'Angelo/Superstar, Wonder Woman, Baa Baa Black Sheep, Police Woman, Hawaii Five-O, The Eddie Capra Mysteries, Quincy M.E., The Rebels, Charlie's Angels, Dallas, Fantasy Island, CHIPS, Simon and Simon, Trapper John M.D., The Love Boat, Riptide, Hardcastle and McCormick, Jake and the Fatman, Laguna Heat, Matlock, The Golden Girls, Murder She Wrote, Dark Justice, Fortune Hunter, Wings, Lover's Knot, Home Improvement, Nash Bridges, The Drew Carey Show, Without a Trace.*

Alvin Ganzer

Alvin Ganzer began his career as an assistant director and later as a second unit director in low budget films in the 1940s. He began directing series television in the early 1950s and worked until the late 1970s.

His TV credits include: *China Smith, Science Fiction Theater, Highway Patrol, Broken Arrow, Alcoa Theater, Zane Grey Theater, Men Into Space, The Twilight Zone, Bonanza, Adventures in Paradise, Ben Casey, Temple Houston, Kraft Suspense Theatre, Route 66, Please Don't Eat the Daisies, Lost in Space, Wild Wild West, The Man from Uncle, Gunsmoke, Cimarron Strip, Hawaii Five-O, The Rookies, Joe Forrester, The Blue Knight, Quincy M.E., The Hardy Boys, Police Woman, The American Girls, David Cassidy-Man Undercover.*

Arthur Hiller

Arthur Hiller sees the affirmation of the human spirit as the key component of a story that attracts him to a film project, and has maintained that perspective since he began his career in radio in the 1950s in *Talks and Public Affairs* at the Canadian Broadcasting Corporation. He soon was directing docu-dramas and then dramas for CBC Television. NBC then coaxed him to Hollywood to direct several of their Matinee Theatre productions.

He followed with many prestigious "Playhouse 90" dramas including *Massacre at Sand Creek* which earned him an Emmy nomination. He quickly became a director of choice for some of the industry's best known series including *Naked City, Alfred Hitchcock Presents, Gunsmoke, Ben Casey* and *Route 66*.

Hollywood's motion picture industry soon beckoned and he began what has become a string of

Arthur Hiller (Cont'd)

highly successful and critically acclaimed films. Some of Hiller's most recognized films include: *The Babe (1992), Outrageous Fortune (1986), Making Love (1981), The In-Laws (1978), Silver Streak (1976), The Man in the Glass Booth (1975), Man of La Mancha (1972), Plaza Suite (1971), Hospital (1971), Love Story (1970)* for which he was honored with a Golden Globe Award as well as an Academy Award nomination, *The Out-Of-Towners (1969)*, and *The Americanization of Emily (1963)*.

He has served two terms as President of the Directors Guild of America, as a member of the Board of Governors, four terms as President of the Academy of Motion Picture Arts and Sciences, and as a member of the National Film Preservation Board of the Library of Congress.

The Academy of Motion Picture Arts and Sciences presented Arthur Hiller with the Jean Hersholt Humanitarian Award at the 74th Annual Academy Awards on March 24, 2002. The award is given to a member of the film community whose humanitarian efforts have been a credit to the industry.

Herbert B. Leonard

Herbert B. Leonard began his career in Hollywood in the late 1940s as a production and unit manager in over 50 low-budget films and action serials. In the mid-50s, he began producing 30-minute television series such as *The Adventures of Rin Tin Tin, Circus Boy, and Tales of the 77th Bengal Lancers*. In the early 1960s he was the executive producer of two memorable television dramas: *Naked City* and *Route 66*. He continued to function as an executive producer and producer on a variety of television projects through

Herbert B. Leonard (Cont'd)

the 1980s. As an executive producer or producer: *Rescue 8, Naked City, Route 66, The Perils of Pauline, Premiere, Popi, Going Home, The Catcher, Nightside, Friendly Persuasion, Sparrow, Ladies Man,* and *Katts and Dog.*

As a production or unit manager (partial list): *The Adventures of Sir Galahad, Mark of the Gorilla, Tyrant of the Sea, Cody of the Pony Express, Captive Girl, State Penitentiary, Pirates of the High Seas, Atom Man vs. Superman, Chain Gang, Last of the Buccaneers, Pygmy Island, Revenue Agent, A Yank in Korea, Fury of the Congo, Mysterious Island, The Magic Carpet, Captain Video, Thunda, Brave Warrior, California Conquest, Blackhawk, The Pathfinder, Savage Mutiny, Serpent of the Nile, Flame of Calcutta, Sky Commando, The Iron Glove, The Miami Story, Riding with Buffalo Bill, Perils of the Wilderness,* and *Blazing the Overland Trail.*

George Maharis

George Maharis was discovered on New York's off-Broadway stage by producer-director Otto Preminger. This led to the role of Yaov in the film *Exodus*. Dark, intense and charismatic, Maharis zoomed to TV stardom on *Route 66* in the early 1960s. Also an accomplished vocalist, he recorded six albums for Columbia Records and had a highly-charted hit single with "Teach Me Tonight." Maharis left *Route 66* during the third season due to illness. In the mid-to-late 60s, he starred and co-starred in seven feature films and seldom appeared on network television. In 1970, he returned to series TV in *The Most Deadly Game*. Through the 1970s and early 1980s he starred and guest-starred in numerous television movies, and episodic dramas. He continued to appear occa-

George Maharis (Cont'd)

sionally until the early 1990s before retiring from acting to concentrate on impressionistic painting.

His feature film work includes: *Exodus, Quick Before It Melts, Sylvia, The Satan Bug, A Covenant with Death, The Happening, The Desperados, Land Raiders, The Sword and the Sorcerer,* and *Doppelganger.* Television credits include: *Alcoa Theater, Naked City, Route 66, Bob Hope Presents the Chrysler Theater, The Danny Thomas Hour, Escape to Mindanao, The Monk, Night Gallery, Cade's County, Medical Center, Cannon, The Victim, Mission Impossible, Barnaby Jones, Shaft, Death in Space, The Snoop Sisters, Thriller, McMillan and Wife, Nakia, Murder on Flight 502, Rich Man-Poor Man, Ellery Queen, Jigsaw John, Bert D'Angelo/Superstar, Look What's Happened to Rosemary's Baby, Gibbsville, The Bionic Woman, SST: Death Flight, Kojak, Police Story, Switch, Return to Fantasy Island, Logan's Run, Crash, Fantasy Island, Matt Houston, Superboy,* and *Murder She Wrote.*

Nancy Malone

Nancy Malone was featured on the cover of the Tenth Anniversary issue of *LIFE* Magazine as "The Typical American Child," but her life, which began in Queens, New York, has been anything but typical. Shortly after she appeared on that cover, Nancy started here acting career, performing on radio and live television. She took formal acting classes at The Stella Adler Conservatory and continued studying with Miss Adler until her death. She currently stuides with Milton Katselas and is a member of the famed Actors Studio. She acted in television's very first soap opera, *The First Hundred Years,* and starred as Libby in the award-winning series *Naked City,* which garnered Nancy her first Emmy nomination. She

Nancy Malone (Cont'd)

won the "Best Performance by an Actress" award from the American Cinema Editors for her portrayal of Clare Varner in the series, *The Long Hot Summer*.

At age sixteen, Nancy made her Broadway debut, co-starring with Melvyn Douglas in *Time Out For Ginger*, for which she received a nomination for a Sarah Siddons Award. She followed this success with *Major Barbara, Requiem For a Heavyweight, A Touch of the Poet, The Chalk Garden*, and *The Trial of the Catonsville Nine*.

On television, Nancy's hundreds of guest star roles began with *U.S. Steel Hour, Studio One, The Hallmark Hall of Fame* and the NBC Special, *A Tree Grows in Brooklyn*. She followed with appearances on *Bonanza, The Fugitive, The Outer Limits, Twilight Zone, Big Valley, Rockford Files* and *The Partridge Family*, to name a few.

In 1971, Nancy realized the need for versatility in the business and she became a story analyst for Tomorrow Entertainment, which led to a position as Director of Motion Pictures, and was then appointed the first woman Vice President of Television at Twentieth Century Fox. It was during this time that Nancy co-founded Women In Film, the most powerful women's organization in Hollywood and now worldwide. She served on its Board of Directors and she continues to work with them, as liaison to the Advisory Council on the Women In Film Foundation Board of Trustees.

With the establishment of Lilac Productions in 1975, she began to produce films for TV. Her credits includes movies of the week, *Winner Take All*, starring Shirley Jones (NBC), *Sherlock Holmes in New York, Like Mom, Like Me* (CBS), and *The Great Pretender* (ABC). She produced the series *Bionic Woman* and won an Emmy Award for *Bob Hope: The First 90 Years*. In 1977,

Nancy Malone (Cont'd)

Nancy was presented with Women In Film's first prestigious Crystal Award.

During the 1980's Nancy Malone completed the American Film Institute's Directing Workshop for Women and began her directing career. Her first full-length film, *There Were Times Dears* (PBS), was also the first film about Alzheimer's disease. This film went on to receive many awards as well as raising over $3,000,000 for caregivers throughout the country.

As a director, Nancy has helmed many top TV shows. Her first episodic directing assignment was the 100th episode of *Dynasty*, where she became an on-staff director. *Knots Landing, Beverly Hills 90210, Sisters, Melrose Place, Cagney and Lacey, Star Trek: Voyager, Touched By an Angel, Dawson's Creek, Judging Amy, The Guardian,* starring Simon Baker, and *Resurrection Boulevard* are a few of the series for which she directed multiple episodes. Additionally she has directed several movies of the week for the networks.

Returning to her theater roots, she has directed *All the Way Home, Agnes of God* and *Prelude To a Kiss* (at L.A. Theatre Works), *Long Day's Journey Into Night, Big Maggie* starring Tyne Daly at the Beverly Hills Playhouse, and *Howie the Rookie* at the Irish Arts Centre, where she received the New York Times Critic's Pick.

Nancy Malone is the recipient of numerous awards, including two Emmys (along with several nominations), a Founders Award from Women In Film, The Nancy Susan Reynolds Award for *Beverly Hills 90210*, and the Cine Golden Eagle, American Film Festival Blue Ribbon and others for *There Were Times Dear.*

Sam Manners

Sam Manners has enjoyed a lengthy career in film and television as a producer, associate producer, executive in charge of production, production manager, and second unit director. His many credits as a producer and associate producer include: *Hawaii Five-O, Valdez is Coming, Powderkeg, Pearl, The Treasure Seekers, Hot Rod, Dummy, Before and After, Guyana Tragedy: The Story of Jim Jones, The Pride of Jesse Hallom, Divorce Wars: A Love Story, Mischief, Bad Medicine, Casanova, Bloodlines: Murder in The Family, Lies of the Heart: The Story of Laurie Kellogg, Beyond Betrayal, A Walton Easter.*

As a production and unit manager, and executive in charge of production, his film and TV credits include: *Rescue 8, Naked City, Route 66, The Wild Wild West, Tarzan and the Valley of Gold, Heaven with a Gun, Mongo's Back in Town, Something Evil, Black Gunn, Cleopatra Jones, The Deadly Trackers, Petrocelli, The Last Hard Men, Sparrow,* and *Going Hollywood.* His son Kim Manners is a well-established executive producer, and a second son Kelly Manners is a successful television producer.

Martin Milner

Martin Milner began his acting career at age 15 when he was cast as John Day in *Life with Father* in 1947. Throughout the 1950s Milner appeared in numerous feature films. In 1960 he was cast as Tod Stiles in *Route 66* and remained with the show until its cancellation in 1964. In 1968 Milner was cast as Officer Pete Malloy in the long-running *Adam-12* TV series produced by Jack Webb. From 1975-1976 Milner starred as Karl Robinson in the short-lived *The Swiss Family Robinson.*

His feature film credits include: *Sands of Iwo Jima, Louisa, Halls of Montezuma, Operation Pacific, Fighting*

Martin Milner (Cont'd)

Coast Guard, I Want You, The Captive City, My Wife's Best Friend, Springfield Rifle, Battle Zone, Last of the Comanches, Destination Gobi, Mister Roberts, Pete Kelly's Blues, Francis in the Navy, On the Threshold of Space, Navy Wife, Screaming Eagles, Pillars of the Sky, Man Afraid, Gunfight at the OK Corral, Sweet Smell of Success, Too Much Too Soon, Marjorie Morningstar, Compulsion, and *Valley of the Dolls.*

His many television credits include: *Schlitz Playhouse of Stars, Dragnet, TV Reader's Digest, Science Fiction Theater, Navy Log, The Life of Riley, West Point, Wagon Train, Rawhide, The Twilight Zone, The Millionaire, Desilu Playhouse, Route 66, Slattery's People, Kraft Suspense Theater, Gidget, Laredo, A Man Called Shenandoah, The Virginian, Twelve O'Clock High, The Rat Patrol, Run for Your Life, Felony Squad, Columbo, Adam-12, Emergency, Flood!, SST: Death Flight, Police Story, Little Mo, Crisis in Mid-Air, The Last Convertible, Fantasy Island, Airwolf, MacGyver, Robocop, Murder She Wrote,* and *Diagnosis Murder.*

Nehemiah Persoff

After training at the Actors Studio with Elia Kazan and later with Lee Strasberg, Nehemiah Persoff made his Broadway debut in *Galileo.* Throughout the 1950s he appeared in numerous Broadway plays, in many live television shows, and in feature films.

In 1960, he joined the group of New York actors who moved to California to work in television. Persoff continued to act in films and also appeared frequently in episodic television, TV movies and mini-series over the next three decades. He retired from acting in the early 1990s to concentrate on painting.

Nehemiah Persoff (Cont'd)

Film credits include: *On the Waterfront, The Harder They Fall, The Wrong Man, Men in War, Street of Sinners, This Angry Age, The Badlanders, Day of the Outlaw, Some Like It Hot, Al Capone, Green Mansions, Never Steal Anything Small, The Big Show, The Comancheros, The Hook, Fate is the Hunter, The Global Affair, The Greatest Story Ever Told, The Power, The Money Jungle, The Girl Who Knew Too Much, Red Sky at Morning, The People Next Door, Voyage of the Damned, Yentil, Twins,* and *The Last Temptation of Christ.*

His many television credits include: *Playhouse 90, Twilight Zone, Wagon Train, Alfred Hitchcock Presents, Naked City, Route 66, The Untouchables, Voyage to the Bottom of the Sea, Thriller, The Dick Powell Theater, The Trials of O'Brien, Rawhide, Ben Casey, Burke's Law, Mr. Novak, I Spy, Honey West, The Legend of Jesse James, The Wild Wild West, The Man from Uncle, A Man Called Shenandoah, The Big Valley, The Time Tunnel, The Flying Nun, Gilligan's Island, Mission Impossible, The Name of the Game, High Chaparral, Gunsmoke, The Mod Squad, Hawaii Five-O, Dan August, The Streets of San Francisco, Marcus Welby M.D., McCloud, Mannix, Love American Style, The Six Million Dollar Man, The Bionic Woman, Cannon, Policy Story, Baretta, Police Woman, The Invisible Man, The Hardy Boys, Quincy M.E., Vegas, Barney Miller, Fantasy Island, Hotel, MacGyver, L.A. Law, Magnum, P.I., Highway to Heaven, Hunter, Law and Order, Star Trek: The Next Generation, Murder She Wrote, Chicago Hope,* and *Reasonable Doubts.*

James Sheldon

James Sheldon was directing the radio show *We, The People,* when it became the first commercial network program to telecast nationally on June 1, 1948. His live TV credits include dramatic series such as

James Sheldon (Cont'd)

Robert Montgomery Presents, Armstrong Circle Theater, Studio One, and comedies like *Mister Peepers.* Sheldon was part of the move from New York to Los Angeles as television product shifted West in the mid-fifties. His numerous series credits include: *West Point Story, Harbor Command, Dick Powell's Zane Grey Theater, Richard Diamond, The Millionaire, Perry Mason, Alfred Hitchcock Presents, Wagon Train, Twilight Zone, My Three Sons, 87th Precinct, Naked City, Route 66, Death Valley Days, Gunsmoke, Walt Disney's Wonderful World of Color, The Virginian, That Girl, Owen Marshall: Counselor at Law, Ironside, MacMillan and Wife, Sanford and Son, Cagney and Lacey,* and *The Equalizer.*

Included in the list of the many actors he helped are James Dean, Paul Newman, Dustin Hoffman, Gene Hackman, Carroll O'Connor, Clint Eastwood, Burt Reynolds, Lee Remick, Robert Loggia and Tyne Daly.

He is currently writing a book highlighting his five-decade career that took him from the Golden Age of TV in New York to film and taped shows in Hollywood, then back to New York again.

Stirling Silliphant

Academy Award winning screenwriter Stirling Silliphant began as an advertising executive in the film industry before beginning a prolific career as a writer in feature films, network television, and later as a novelist. His film credits include: *Damn Citizen, The Lineup, The Slender Thread, In the Heat of the Night, Charley, Marlowe, The Liberation of L. B. Jones, Walk in the Spring Rain, Murphy's War, The New Centurions, The Poseidon Adventure, Shaft in Africa, The Towering Inferno, The Killer Elite, The Enforcer, Telefon, The Swarm, Circle of Iron, When Time Ran Out, Over the Top, Catch*

Stirling Silliphant (Cont'd)

the Heat, Salween, Village of the Damned, The Grass Harp. Television: *Zane Grey Theater, Perry Mason, Suspicion, Alfred Hitchcock Presents, Rawhide, Tightrope, Mr. Lucky, Naked City, Route 66, Bob Hope Presents the Chrysler Theater, Longstreet, The New Healers, Movin' On, A Time for Love, The First 36 Hours of Dr. Durant, Death Scream, Pearl, Fly Away Home, Golden Gate, Travis McGee, Space, Mussolini: The Untold Story, A Stranger in the Mirror,* and *Day of Reckoning.*

ENDNOTES

1. Herbert B. Leonard, Sam Manners, and Stirling Silliphant. From Richard Maynard's interviews in *Emmy* Magazine, September/October 1982.
2. Richard Maynard, from his article in *Emmy* Magazine, September/October 1982.
3. Mark Alvey, telephone interview by author. Chicago, IL, July 2006.
4. Martin Milner, George Maharis, and Sam Manners. From Kermit Park's interviews in *Corvette Quarterly*, Summer 1990.
5. George Maharis, telephone interview by the author. Los Angeles, CA, July 2006.
6. Sam Manners, telephone interview by the author. Los Angeles, CA, July 2006.
7. Arthur Hiller, telephone interview by the author. Los Angeles, CA, July 2006.
8. Alvin Ganzer, telephone interview by the author. Hawaii, June 2006.
9. Nancy Malone, telephone interview by the author. Los Angeles, CA, June 2006.
10. James Sheldon, interview by the author. New York City, May 2006.
11. Nehemiah Persoff, telephone interview by the author. Los Angeles, CA June 2006.
12. Anne Francis, telephone interview by the author. Los Angeles, CA, July 2006.

ABOUT THE AUTHOR

(Courtesy of The Reporter)

Born and raised in Northwest Philadelphia, James Rosin graduated from Temple University's School of Communications with a degree in broadcasting. In New York, he studied acting with Bobby Lewis and appeared in plays off-off Broadway and on the ABC soap opera, *Edge of Night*. In Los Angeles, Rosin played featured and costarring roles in such TV shows as *Mike Hammer, T. J. Hooker, Quincy M.E., The Powers of Matthew Star, Cannon, Mannix, Banacek, Adam-12, Love, American Style,* and two miniseries, *Loose Change* and *Once an Eagle*. He also wrote stories and teleplays for *Qunicy M.E.* (NBC), *Capitol* (CBS), and *Loving Friends and Perfect Couples* (Showtime). His full-length play, *Michael in Beverly Hills*, premiered at American Theater Arts in Los Angeles and was later

Cont'd on next page

presented off-off Broadway, at the American Musical Dramatic Academy's Studio One Theater.

In recent years, Rosin has written and produced two one-hour sports documentaries, which have aired on public television: *Philly Hoops: The SPHAS and Warriors* (about the first two professional basketball teams in Philadelphia) and *The Philadelphia Athletics 1901-1954* (about the former American League franchise). His first book, *Philly Hoops: The SPHAS and Warriors*, was published in October of 2003 followed by *Rock, Rhythm & Blues*, in September 2004. His third book, *Philadelphia: City of Music*, debuted in May of 2006.